INTERPERSONAL PSYCHOANALYSIS
New Directions

INTERPERSONAL PSYCHOANALYSIS
New Directions

Edited by

EARL G. WITENBERG, M.D.
The William Alanson White Institute

GARDNER PRESS, INC., NEW YORK

Distributed by Halsted Press
Division of John Wiley & Sons, Inc.

NEW YORK ● LONDON ● SYDNEY ● TORONTO

GARDNER PRESS, INC.
19 Union Square West
New York, New York 10003

Distributed solely by the Halsted Press
Division of John Wiley & Sons, Inc., New York

Library of Congress Cataloging in Publication Data
Main entry under title:

Interpersonal psychoanalysis.

    Includes index.
    1. Psychoanalysis—Addresses, essays, lectures.
I. Witenberg, Earl G.
RC509.I53   616.8917   78-902
ISBN 0-470-26318-0

Printed in the United States of America

INTRODUCTION

PSYCHOANALYSIS—its theories and its practice—undergoes continuous change. It reflects the novel findings and new formulations of fields as disparate as neurophysiology and social or cultural theory or philosophy. It treats types of people for whom the approach seemed closed 25 and 30 years ago. It generates new data which have been applied not only to itself but also to other fields. Analysts have influenced the teachings in psychiatry, medicine, psychology, social science, and law.

It seemed appropriate then for the William Alanson White Institute to offer a course in its Continuing Professional Education Division which would make current the seminal thinking of some of its senior members. The chapters in this volume are an outcome of that course; by and large these pages represent modifications and additions to the material presented.

These chapters are not intended to be read sequentially. Since all the authors are practicing clinicians, the reader will find clinical material interspersed in all the papers. The first chapter, by Marianne Horney Eckardt, describes what she wants to achieve in therapy and how she goes about reaching her goals. The chapters by Jerome L. Singer and Edward S. Tauber attempt to show how their research in other areas, daydreams and the sleep-waking cycles, have influenced their therapeutic approaches. David E. Schecter brings to fruition his many years of study of the nature of attachment bonds and of relatedness and demonstrates the impact these studies have had on his work with patients. In an intriguing chapter, Silvano Arieti explicates his nearly 40 years of work, his entry into the area of schizophrenia, the influence of the interpersonal approach of the White Institute, his addition of the cognitive substrate and the intrapsychic dimension to this approach, and how he arrived in the area of creativity. Gerard Chrzanowski, in a theoretical-clinical paper, adds to his exposition of the self and shows how his heuristic, open-ended approach favorably influences therapy. In his search to understand the nature of change in analysis, Edgar A. Levenson brings to bear his understanding of linguistics and shows how the dialectic between metaphor and metonymy can be used to explain the change in the patient during psychoanalysis. He offers this approach to the psychoanalytic process—a language process, or more properly a semiotic process—as a way of obviating the charges that analysis is persuasion or indoctrination.

All these authors subscribe to a certain set of assumptions. They would all agree that there are broadening and changing indications for the kind of person to whom psychoanalysis is applicable. What this implies is that treatment must be tailored to the individual. Today's analyst needs to have a flexible approach. As times have changed, so have the problems for which people seek relief. So the belief is that in an intensive relationship with an expert an individual can become what he might have been if such and such events had not happened to him during his lifetime. Other givens are that experiences not attended to, or dissociated or repressed, result in a distorted view of matters or in untoward behavior. Dreams, bodily sensations, cognitive styles, and values, as well as language, are used to discover the unknown.

Different kinds of psychoanalytic theories are used to incorporate these data. The following categorization is heuristic.

1. Some theories attempt a theory of man as a whole. They present explicit statements about the ultimate nature of man. They attempt to show the relation between biology and psychology—and make psychological phenomena dependent upon assumed biological phenomena. Freudian theory in its original version and Erich Fromm's later thinking belong in this category.

2. Other theories attempt to articulate what they have found from the psychoanalytic method. Although they do not assume the person is a *tabula rasa,* they state that only psychological issues can be discovered by the analytic method. Thus this approach does not allow inferences from the biological. These theories tend to correlate and interrelate social and cultural phenomena with the psychological. Horney, Sullivan, Erikson, Thompson, early Fromm and ego-psychology fall in this category.

3. Recently numerous theories have appeared that draw heavily from other fields and attempt to incorporate them into the analytic

schema. Such theories attempt to apply general systems theory to psychoanalysis. Among the areas subsumed here are structuralism, linguistics, and approaches such as those advanced by Ardrey, Lorenz, and Wilson. Lacan, Edelson, and Schafer are analysts associated with the linguistic approaches to analysis.

The influence of new findings from the observational area as well as from the theoretical sphere is apparent in the work of all analysts. Findings from ethology, infant development, and personal development have demonstrated that the individual actively influences his environment from the first days of life. As will be noted in this volume, most analysts assume the patient has more responsibility for the predicament in which he finds himself than analysts would have assumed twenty years ago. More attention is being paid to issues arising from attachment and separation.

There is also more emphasis on the positive and the productive aspects of his life that the patient brings into treatment. Behavior is no longer considered "nothing but" a repetition of the past, although at times it may be. Helping people to understand their value systems has become an important part of treatment today.

It is also more clearly understood today than previously that changes occur after adolescence in the individual's development. These changes have to do with the individual's life circumstances as well as with the time-of-life (e.g., middle age, old age). Different facets of personality, different attitudes and experience are drawn upon in raising a family, in living alone, in choosing to live alone or in being forced to live alone, in beginning, ending, or changing a career. All these circumstances influence both the content and the process of treatment.

Analyses tend to proceed with a painstaking exploration of the individual transactions, their context and content. Then, because of a change in the structure of the memory, or the impact of additional information, a modification of the attitude, behavior, or perception under scrutiny occurs.

In order to help the patient pay attention to the issues involved, the analyst uses his own attitudes and behavior to encourage the patient's cooperation. The real aspects of the analyst's activities that encourage a working relationship are those related to his curiosity and his willingness to explore emotionally laden areas. His well-meaning stance and his regard for the patient's self-esteem and predicament enhance this working alliance. Treatment is thus seen as more than overcoming resistance; it is a joint effort toward making both participants more human.

In general, the authors in this volume share the above view of theories and of treatment. By no means, however, would they agree with all the specifics of the formulation. As you read the chapters, you will be impressed by the vitality of the observations. You will perceive how the indications for psychoanalysis have both broadened and become more refined; at the same time you will observe how complicated the human being has become. A person is no longer viewed as merely in the grips of his instinctual drives; nor is he merely the result of his social and cultural environment. He is seen as a shaper of his environment from early in life. In the therapeutic context he can become aware of the resources he has had all along—his perceptions, his thoughts, his affects, and his body. He is considered to have the potential for growth and development, limited only by his biological givens. All the authors indicate how treatment is more than lifting repressions and developing insight. For David Schecter, the therapeutic attitude is one of curiosity and exploration rather than explanation and interpretation. For the others, I suspect it would be a blend of the two.

You will notice the absence of psychoanalytic jargon in this volume. The reason is that psychoanalytic terms come to mean something other than their original definitions (and the modifications exist side by side with the original meanings); they also tend to become reified and are assumed to have more than a metaphoric existence. Moreover, some of the authors' interventions are not in the classical mode—they affirm their patients' statements, reflect their own feelings, or ask for fantasy productions directly. By combining experience with meaning, these authors are placing analysis on a different footing from that of the past.

Editing this book has been a genial task. I know there are other members of the White Institute who might have contributed, but this is a statement of an actual class in the Continuing Professional Education Division. We owe the members of that Division our thanks, with special acknowledgment to Dale Ortmeyer, Ph.D., its Director.

—Earl G. Witenberg, M.D.

CONTRIBUTORS

Silvano Arieti, M.D.
Training and Supervising Analyst, William Alanson White Institute
Clinical Professor of Psychiatry, New York Medical College
Associate Attending Psychiatrist, Metropolitan Hospital

Gerard Chrzanowski, M.D.
Training and Supervising Analyst, William Alanson White Institute
Associate Clinical Professor of Psychiatry, New York Medical College
Medical Director, Bleuler Psychotherapy Center

Marianne Horney Eckardt, M.D.
Past President, The American Academy of Psychoanalysis
Associate Clinical Professor of Psychiatry, New York Medical College,
     Division of Psychoanalysis

Edgar A. Levenson, M.D.
Director of Clinical Services, Fellow, Training and Supervising Analyst,
     William Alanson White Institute
Associate Clinical Professor of Psychiatry, Albert Einstein College of Medicine

David E. Schecter, M.D.
Fellow, Training and Supervising Analyst, William Alanson White Institute
Associate Clinical Professor, Albert Einstein College of Medicine

Jerome L. Singer, Ph.D.
Professor of Psychology, Director, Clinical Psychology Training Program,
     Yale University

Edward S. Tauber, M.D.
Fellow, Training and Supervising Analyst, Senior Consultant,
     Psychophysiological Research, William Alanson White Institute
Research Consultant, Department of Neurology and Psychiatry,
     Montefiore Hospital and Medical Center

Earl G. Witenberg, M.D.
Director, Fellow, Training and Supervising Analyst,
     William Alanson White Institute.
Associate Clinical Professor of Psychiatry, Albert Einstein College of Medicine

CONTENTS

1

BELIEFS AND REFLECTIONS
OF A THERAPIST

MARIANNE HORNEY ECKARDT, M.D.

I HAVE agreed to do the impossible: to write what I am all about in doing therapy. The emphasis will not be on theory, nor on clinical syndromes, techniques, or our changing philosophical notions. I have no enticing new technique or dynamic formula of a particular syndrome to offer. Instead I hope to impart my particular flavor of doing therapy. I will write about myself, my way of thinking about life, about our *condition humaine,* about my way of seeing troubled people, about ideas that matter to me and thus flavor my therapeutic activity.

Biologically we are social beings. We need a social frame to order or facilitate order in our existence. Above all we need some affirmation of our perceptions, for only then do they take on enough substance to be available for integration into concepts, beliefs, impressions, or convictions.

A brief clinical vignette will enliven this statement. A very bright youngster emerged from a troubled childhood into a period of passionate political and sexual aliveness at age 12. Her rebellious behavior was called "sick". She had some unfortunate, undermining psychiatric attention, and then, through the death of one parent and the remarriage of the other, she lost a welcoming home. She felt she was not allowed to *be.* "I had the fantasy of dying young, metaphorically speaking," she said. "People did not accept me for what I was. I was not to feel what I felt, not to know what I knew. Even obvious truth was denied." She went into years of blank detachment, half alive, hardly even suffering. She developed a facade to get by. Her face looked sadly old and missed the spark of youth. When I saw her, she was 16. She emerged only slowly to feel and communicate the true poignancy of her feelings and thoughts, past and present.

As mentioned, thoughts, feelings, and perceptions remain unformed, unavailable for conceptual use unless they find validation in some social reflection. By validation I mean no more than that somewhere in the world of mankind one encounters similar experiences. Books, drama, myths, fairy tales, music, or the sharing of thoughts of others—all are potential sources for giving our perceptions the right to "be."

Isolation, if this includes isolation from people, their rituals and creative products, is inimical to a sense of aliveness. It does more than starve the mind and senses; it disorganizes our mental functioning.

Thus one of my therapeutic activities is a special kind of listening. It is a listening that tries to separate what was truly perceived and what was borrowed or constructed after the fact. I freely explore to get a sense of what rings true, sometimes with success and often just aware that, for the time being, I do not know. Perceptions undergo secondary elaborations or intellectualizations very rapidly. The third sentence of a spontaneous description of an event may contradict the more immediate first sentence. My patients hear me say over and over again, "Rely on your own perceptions. It is all you have to go by. It is not a matter of being right or wrong; they reflect where you happen to be, and you can go on from there. You may change your impressions by further experience, which we call learning. If you rely on what 'one' thinks, or 'he' says, or 'I the therapist' say, either you will continue to believe that others know more about your perceptions than you, which is not helpful, or you will discover that other peoples' estimate was wrong, and you continue to flounder."

Part of my effort to respect patients' own perceptions and help their sense of validation is that I try to know the details of a past or present troublesome situation. I ask questions that allow me to visualize the particulars and the atmosphere as clearly as possible. Free associations are valuable for the reasons stated in the literature, but they omit much we therapists need to know for satisfactory visualization, for the patient takes for granted what is familiar to him, and our only good guide is our total curiosity.

I am fairly free with responses to what I hear, be they empathetic, puzzling, or challenging. I view my responsiveness as a dialogue, not an interpretation, and certainly not as telling the patient what to do; as a dialogue that is a necessary social context for the patient to clarify his thoughts and feelings. While I aim to understand right, a wrong response of mine may clarify as much as a more accurate one would have done. By knowing what is not, we sometimes know what is. But knowing what one perceives is just the first step. I make a clear distinction between experiencing a feeling and action. Perception acknowledged permits further exploration. The question of action or expression always involves a larger context of appropriateness. I apologize for this self-evident statement, but simplistic notions of communication or expression of feelings for their own sake as a valuable enterprise are still much in vogue.

I believe in the individual's uniqueness,—uniqueness in the sense that no two living beings are ever totally alike. Our bodies and their chemistry are different; so is our way of perceiving, our sensitivities, the things that matter, our gifts, flairs, inclinations, and temperament. By uniqueness I do not mean exceptionality, but a quality, a flavor that is distinct. This is a precious possession. It constitutes what at times we experience as our identity. The words "identity" and "self-realization" have been bandied about a great deal to no one's benefit. They have contributed to a cult of individualism where each person, asocial and self-centered, wants to be different at all costs, in opposition to others; often such individuals aggressively assert their domain, yet at the same time desire tribute from those they do not respect. By uniqueness I mean what is simply there in all of us, to be equally appreciated and respected in others as well as in ourselves.

More than anything else, uniqueness is the spice, the joys of many hues, as well as the sorrows and the disappointments. It is the gamut we call the meaning of life. I am talking about many little things. I love the spectacular view of the East River from my window, as if from the captain's bridge on a boat. The birds and brightly striped boats, the blues or greys, the crisp or foggy sky, all change to make the scene ever new. Several chimneys spout huge streams of white smoke. I know it is pollution, but that is not what I think of. The white stream draws lines in the sky, sometimes meandering lazily straight upward, at other times lashed horizontally by the wind and dissolving in ever-varying forms. It is there for me to see. I drive in my little Toyota up the FDR Drive to my office. Sometimes I am content to be stuck peacefully behind a slowpoke car. I can dream along or attend to thinking and not worry about the traffic. Other times the little stretch becomes a game. I weave just enough to keep up my speed and am slightly victorious over having gotten the best of some other car. Then there are the red lights. They can stop me four times along the way, and there is precious little I can do about their occurrence or nonoccurrence. Sometimes I feel smiled on by fate as only one red light stops my progress.

Very rarely am I triumphantly ushered through, green lights all the way.

These are little inconsequential games. René Dubos (1972) describes an aspect of child development: "Increasingly, furthermore, the child tries to create a world, external and conceptual, in which to discover himself. Play can be regarded as the chief method children use for securing the kinds of sensation and perceptions out of which they construct their private reality" (p. 76).

Play and the play of fantasy continue into adulthood. With talent and work, play emerges in creative art. It finds some expression in adults' games. I want to emphasize its presence in the thousand ways we conduct the usual activities of our lives. Pleasure and fantasy can enter into cooking, eating, a walk in the woods or along the beach, watching the sandpipers scurrying before us. The meaning of movement in dance, of sound patterns in music, of beauty in the spoken word varies forever in poignancy for each individual. Joy and disappointment belong together. Meaning sometimes is a happening, unanticipated, a present offered by life. Usually meaning is the motivating force to create the opportunity for enrichment.

What does all this have to do with therapy?

It is a dimension we have to pay as much attention to as we do to signs of what we call neurotic defenses, mechanisms, or trends. Most of our patients have curtailed their sense of aliveness. Many have emptied their life of meaning. Let us be sure to find out where meaning still exists, where it did exist, when it was cut off, and under what circumstances.

Patients first tell us what troubles them. We gradually hear more about family and friends or enemies, about work, loneliness, and isolation. It takes quite a while before we come to know the many little things, the little passions, the more private world of the individual.

Freud, of course, made us aware of the negative repercussions of repressed sexuality and sensuality. Jung broadened Freud's concept of vital energy. He led our attention to the realm of myths, imagination, and art. Yet our preoccupation with pathology, its causes and mechanisms, has made us inattentive to the manifold ways in which we enliven our private reality. In fact, our reductionistic theories have stereotyped rather than individualized people in spite of their therapeutic aim of personal unfolding.

I do explore this private dimension. I pursue, as you do, the necessary missing connections to a pathological phenomenon. I need to make sense out of what I hear. I know that a logic of patterns is there if I just go on looking. I am equally interested, however, in what I call the unique flavor in all its manifestations. So we do talk about books, hobbies, tastes, styles, food, and whatever. Nature for many is a non-ending harbor of peace, of physical and mental revitalization. But even this resource is often neglected. I will let another clinical vignette express my thoughts.

I discover that one of my patients owns a horse. Does she enjoy riding? "Oh, yes." Does she ride often? No, she has not ridden for two years. Her mild depression or unhappiness dates back at least that long. But it was not just that her spirits were dampened because of tensions in her family. We see a whole trend of anti-enjoyment. No quiet time for herself, no reading of a pleasurable book, no fun-parties, no walk in the nearby woods. Did she ever have periods of aliveness? Oh, yes, there were periods of intense sparkle. Her early life and adolescence were burdened with much isolation and greyness, but even then, from early on, she was a child of intense perceptions, of knowing that her parents made no sense. She fought for what appeared right to her. She assumed an excess of responsibility as they would not or could not do their share. She argued to convince others and to make them see. Here, then, I knew she had a keen vitality and perceptiveness, an in-born wiseness, and also a capacity for joy. In the partial warfare of a personal relationship she lost some of her spirit, protected herself by a determined self-reliance, and resignedly accepted the existence of incompetent, irrational others. She talked to me at a furious rate to pour out her thoughts and feelings, neither expecting nor allowing me to respond to what she had to say. Whatever I did therapeutically addressed itself to her present troubled way of being, but invariably also to what I had sensed of her vitality, sparkle, and particular quality of knowingness. Therapy, I believe, was effective, because I enjoyed what she had to say, I enjoyed her common sense and her courage of her own convictions. Whatever wisdom I may have had to offer was purely incidental in the process.

Many patients, as a consequence of interpersonal troubles leading to neurotic reaction patterns, will empty their lives of meaning. A lover deserts, a marriage goes dead, a companion dies, a meaningful productive work situation dissolves, and all color, taste, meaning recede from life. Depression is prototypical, and so is pervasive anxiety. It matters little what the anxiety is all about. Like a pervasive pain, it centers life on the pain and not on life. The obsessive-compulsive, too, forever riding the two horses of doing and negation at the same time, is much too busy with his agitated "yes—but" to let life penetrate to a level of real meaning.

Let us be aware, though, of our great talent and inclination for generalization. We speak or think about the holistic nature of neurosis. The most enticing version of the holistic nature of neurotic character structure has been brilliantly conceptualized by Andras Angyal in his book *Neurosis and Treatment—A Holistic Theory* (1965). His main theme is briefly: Every whole is organized according to some leading principle. Consequently, we must begin by defining the leading principle in the organization of the process of life. Although a personality must be viewed as a multivalent, pluralistic organization, there nevertheless exists a basic difference in the overall organization we call "healthy," as compared to the one we call "neurotic." The organization of the neurotic system bears the imprint of its origin in the state of isolation and anxiety; several features present defects of integration along with the dimensions of depth, progression, and breadth. The world of the healthy feels like one's home; it is rich in opportunities, lawfully ordered, and meaningfully related to the person. Angyal's special contribution is his concept of universal ambiguity. In each neurotic the neurotic and healthy systems coexist, but, as in figure-ground perception, one system is dominant at any one time. If the neurotic system is dominant, all is neurotic; if the healthy mode is dominant, the productive mode is dominant. The dual organization is mainly recognized when a shift occurs. Angyal is referring here to a very important phenomenon, which I have often witnessed. One day the patient will give me an account of an inner-outer happening with a maze of neurotic distortions. The next day he will be clear as a bell, with a refined perspective that just seems right, always spoken with calmness and self-assurance. I shall come back to the importance of the concept of our organizing and structuring experience. At the moment, however, I wish to state that in my experience, although neurotic patterns can be pervasive, more often they dominate certain areas of living but leave other areas of functioning completely unaffected. These well-functioning areas are significant. They give us a sense of the potentiality of love, knowledge, islands of well-being and freedom, quiet talents for organization or creative flair. Once you know a person's capacity for meaningful functioning, you also have a better feel for the self-restrictiveness in the areas of dysfunction.

Basically I have found that I have had to separate theories of neurotic development from my clinical perceptions. Only in the beginning hours of getting to know a patient, when I try to build a structure with little information, do the patterns I see tend to conform with classical descriptions. The more I come to know the patient, the less the standard version fits and the more the individual version alone has relevance. The notion of pathology also dims in what becomes a human story with its own struggles and its own means of coping.

I have never liked the concepts of normality or pathology in our theories of neuroses. They seem too black and white. I do not see the child as a passive victim of the environment, and I am against any blaming of parents or other circumstances for the shortcomings in our living. Life and people have been complex and difficult since Adam and Eve. Each culture and each generation brings its own particular stresses. I have seen patients emerge with utmost integrity of self out of impossible circumstances, and others get enmeshed to their own detriment. In spite of all our passion for explanation, there remains something we have to call fate. There remains an accidental choice in our particular mode of adjustment or coping, for the same circumstances provide many options of reacting. That, however, is as far as my fatalism goes, for I see the child as a very active partner in his own personality development.

Let me quote René Dubos (1972) again:

> From the first day of life, the child perceives his environment, stores information about it, and develops patterns of response that become a permanent part of his organic being. Even in the early phase, awareness of environment is not entirely passive, since it is an expression of the biological urge to explore—a curiosity that is universal in its general manifestations but takes forms peculiar to the organism. Very soon the responses to environmental stimuli become conscious and are converted into creative processes; the child behaves as if he were selectively exploring the world around him with some kind of purpose in mind.
>
> Children differ, of course, and each tends to select the environmental conditions best suited to his innate endowment. Increasingly, furthermore, the child tries to create a world, external and conceptual, in which to discover himself (p. 175).

Many a defense, which we conceptualize as stemming from anxiety, did not arise out of anxiety at all, but originated, after some experimentation, from a well-remembered tactical consideration. Many a later attitude of seeming pleasing or conforming arose out of a decision that it is better policy to appear to go along, keeping one's own council, than to allow others to intrude with nagging criticism, advice, or hysteria. These decisions often make eminent sense, given the environmental conditions. Hardened into attitudes, they lead to secrecy, a troublesome compliance, lack of self-direction, and a seeming ego weakness. Anxiety is often a secondary manifestation, arising when the urge to avoid confrontation clashes with a growing intolerance of whatever corner one has been cornered in. Such patients do not necessarily have a weak ego. To me, it is very important to trace the manner in which a non-adaptive or neurotic attitude arises. Often anxiety, resignation, and tactical decisions all play a part; at other times one of these alone may propel a pattern into exisence, and each is a distinctly different inner experience.

Adolescence is a great time for such decisions. I always inquire about diaries and poetry written at any time during the patient's life, but particularly during his adolescence. It is an interesting though inconsequential observation that so many adolescents have written poetry or diaries and then write no more once they become adults. Have we stereotyped adulthood and maturity and socialized the demonic or the transcendental at the expense of our contact with the nonrational, with poetry, myths, plays? Some adolescents are truly in no-man's land, and life does not exist as a meaningful structure or a meaningful self; lonely adolescents pour their intensity into a world of their own making. Diaries are still written and so is poetry; private passions still exist. Some adolescents still cry out in pain; many teeter on the brink of resignation; and others have given up. They become diffuse, obscure to others and themselves.

The following lines are from the diary of a youth not yet 20, who sees the threat of going dead inside, yet in protest flings himself into the fullness of his senses. Some of the metaphor belongs to riding a horse.

How many of us take life and build a casket out of it? How many penthouses in the clouds, and how little song in the street? How many hours and rooms of solitude does it take to make a prism of manufactured and packaged loneliness into a neat ironed and starched picture of life? How much can we capture—how safe can we be, before we fall asleep with nothing else to wean?

I will try to keep up with each inspiration and touch each glimpse, hold each vision in between my teeth and jump through nightmares like windows. I will let the wind howl as it blows through my ears and nose and I will stroke the gestures I love and drink the caresses as they are beheld and my body will follow—it will not dictate—only when we lose shall we stop waving in the breeze like a banner—then we resign from the race and join the other team again. Yes, the right of desire is deep with shadows and lurking reminders—the wind with its quick touch softens his solitude as he rides his horse along.

I started out by talking about the many unique passions and meanings. Adolescence can be a terribly important time. Have we paid enough attention to it? When meaning is at its most intense, as yet unformed, untried, then it is at its most vulnerable. Yes, by that time a personality has already formed for many years. Yet many a deep resignation, a marginal adjustment, or a sacrifice of self follows the intensity which is here to be seen. No, adolescent rebellion and turmoil have no perspective. Adolescence is intensely personal, and its emotions create and see its own high drama—it is what we often call romantic. But in all of its rawness, it contains a core that is still close to real human values. It knows lies, hypocrisy, and being misunderstood. It wants to be seen, heard, allowed to be, acknowledged, and loved; and it knows the visceral pain when hopes are shattered, reaching-out ignored, or efforts negated. For some reason we do not seem to use the word "disappointment" too readily. Disappointment can be devastating; it can be all-negating, especially when an event had gathered into itself all hope and meaning and sense of being. If the world denies, ignores, belittles, and ridicules, then a conviction of pointlessness, of what is the use, or that nothing matters easily takes over, often with a vengeance.

We grow up and learn to adapt, to cope, to develop a persona. The neurotic propensities which in the early twenties hover at the crossroads of life can diminish or can take roots and forms as the person evolves into his or her thirties.

One way of conceiving our task of undoing what we call "neuroses" is that, by whatever psychotherapeutic techniques, we open the person to new experiences, to new explorations, which reflect a willingness to risk the unknown fate. Control, security, and guarantee are not what life has to offer. Another way of conceiving the same task is that we facilitate the person's getting in touch with the meaning and values that once existed in his perception but were befogged in the process of adaptation and we make them available for a restructuring of the person's way of living. Meaning and values, too, are the basic guidelines for our share of effort which imparts to our social existence a sense of partnership.

There is more method in my choice of emphasis than may appear. My conceptualizations of personality functioning have a great affinity to the school of thought Silvano Arieti (1974) described in his *American Handbook of Psychiatry* as "The Cognitive-Volitional School." As I do not like the principle of an ideological school of thought, I prefer to say merely that my thinking starts with the basic premise that there is no biological unit, no cell, no organ, no aspect of a being, no total being without a functional organization. Perceptions are immediately organized into experience, into a pattern that has some sort of meaning and permits functional orientation. Arieti states that a stress on cognition and volition implies that at the human level all feelings except the most primitive are consequent to meaning and choice. However, meaning and choice and feeling again depend on how we view people, the world, and ourselves. Our views are patterned by many factors, by the culture, but always by a process that Susanne Langer (1942) calls our symbol-making function, which is a primary activity of man, a fundamental, ongoing process of the mind. Good functioning has a lot to do with meaningful functional organization. Knowing what matters, values, and beliefs are essential organizing factors in how we behave and direct our life.

Our psychoanalytic theories dwell on pathological structure and organization. We know the power of this kind of organization on thought, feeling, and action. Yet normality is conceived as an absence of pathology, and little thought has been given to the rather intricate organization involved in so-called normal living. We have been very good at breaking old patterns and eliciting feelings held in abeyance, yet from there on out we have assumed that without repression, without denial, the psyche would take care of itself.

But meaning and value, when recognized, need to be integrated as active organizing factors in our life style if they are to be effective. Some patients are marvelous, in fact amazing, in their ability to immediately integrate and act on a perspective once clarified. Others only slowly grow into an exploration of existing possibilities. They have difficulties grasping their actual role in life for good or bad. They lack the imagination to experiment with life events from many angles to arrive at a perspective that is right for them. Others, especially those who have a lifelong tendency to blend with others, or to function in symbiotic dependence, have incredible difficulty in adhering to a system of priorities even though they have already discovered the delightful freedom of living out of their own center.

Good functioning is so varied that no blueprint is possible. A few important considerations exist, however. As mentioned, in spite of the ever-variedness of our activities, there exists something one may call "a philosophy of life." It imparts to each activity and relationship a meaningful connection to whatever is our unique gestalt, and a sense of purposiveness, however undefined. It serves as a perspective to which we can return when moods or disappointments produce enough turmoil to cloud our vision.

Another factor is time, an essential ingredient of any good functioning. A lot of people are at odds with time. Events, our own needs, relationships, all have to have their space in time. Rushing, hecticness, no time for thought, no time for simply doing nothing are not conducive to meaningful activity. Quality of anything has its very specific demands for time, care, and concentration. New York, which I call the rat-race city, poses a never-ending challenge to balance our particular requirements for work and recreation, privacy and sociability.

Then there is the care of our physical health. Our American culture is poor in even minimum rituals for appropriate physical health. Many a fatigue, many an ache and pain, and many an emotional disturbance could be avoided by better attention to our physical needs and a greater awareness that body and mind are an inseparable unit. My own experience has led me to believe that the persistence of neurotic patterns can be due as much to the absence of a new pattern of being as to the rigid hold of the past. I say *can,* which means I have seen many a patient who is visibly anchored in the imagery of the past. But I have also seen others, nonfunctional for many years, who respond to new vistas in an amazingly short time, as if we had given them a new lease on life. This need not be a matter for argument. My therapy is never one-dimensional. I do, though, believe that we should not underestimate our patients' capacity for moving forward. Either they do or they do not; if they do not, we work all the harder.

Let me rephrase this thought to connect with the theme with which I began this chapter. We are social beings, and our perceptions need some echo to stay alive and gain significance for integration into the function of a patient's life. Many a pathological defense may drop away if we address ourselves to that which is meaningful to the person. Integrating meaning and value into normal living is at times a natural propensity in a patient, but most of the time it requires a growth process of trial and error, of exploration, venturing, and imagination.

REFERENCES

Angyal, A. (1965), *Neurosis and Treatment.* New York: Viking.
Arieti, S. (1974), The cognitive-volitional school. In: *American Handbook of Psychiatry,* 2nd ed., 1:877–903. New York: Basic Books.
Dubos, R. (1972), *A God Within.* New York: Scribner.
Langer, S. (1942), *Philosophy in a New Key.* New York: A Mentor Book, The New American Library, p. 45.

2

FROM SCHIZOPHRENIA
TO CREATIVITY

SILVANO ARIETI, M.D.

WHEN AS a young man I escaped from Fascist Italy in 1939 and arrived in this country, without knowing a word of English, I was fortunate to obtain a fellowship and work in the Department of Neuropathology of the New York Psychiatric Institute. I did some research in neuropathology and learned some English; but my main interest was in clinical psychiatry. When the fellowship expired after two years, I became a resident at Pilgrim State Hospital and immediately became involved with the study and treatment of schizophrenia.

The relevance of thought disorders in schizophrenia has been one of my basic concerns from the beginning of my psychiatric studies. Actually the origin of such interest is much more remote in time than my reading of Eugen Bleuler's writings. It goes back to my studies of the eighteenth-century philosopher Giambattista Vico while I was in college. Vico's study of the cognitive ways in which the ancients, the primitives, children, poets conceive of the world and respond to it fascinated me. It initiated my interest in the many possible ways by which the mind faces, reconstructs, and experiences the universe. In my opinion, Vico's conceptions were among the best preparations for understanding the schizophrenic reality and the schizophrenic experience. My discovery of the writings of the psychologist Heinz Werner, shortly after my arrival in America, also helped me to evaluate the full relevance of cognition and directed me toward a comparative developmental approach, for which Vico's writings had already prepared me.

In the time spent at Pilgrim State Hospital, first as a resident and later as a staff psychiatrist from November 1941 to February 1946, I made what seemed to me interesting observations. I discovered that a few patients, who resided in back buildings and had been considered hopeless, would apparently recover or improve enough to be discharged, sometimes after many years of hospitalization. At that time these were considered cases of "spontaneous recovery". I was not satisfied with this explanation and looked more deeply into the matter. I soon discovered that these so-called spontaneous recoveries were not spontaneous at all, but the result of a relationship between the patient and an attendant or nurse. Although I made these observations only in services of female patients, I assumed that the same situation could take place in male services. The relationship went through two stages. In the first stage, by giving the patient special consideration and care, the nurse or attendant met some of her needs, no matter how primitive they were. The patient improved somewhat and the nurse developed attachment and deep involvement with her. The patient soon became the nurse's pet. In the second stage the patient was able to help the nurse with the work on the ward. (These were war years, with acute scarcity of personnel, and any help was very welcome.) The patient would then be praised, and an exchange of approval, affection, and reliability was established. In this climate of exchange of warmth and concern the patient improved to the point of being suitable for discharge. Much to my regret, however, I almost invariably observed that these formerly regressed patients would soon relapse and be readmitted to the hospital. Outside they were not able to "make it".

Nevertheless, I was impressed by the fact that even an advanced schizophrenic process proved reversible or capable of being favorably influenced by a human contact. These were quite advanced notions at that time. I thought that perhaps methods could be devised by which we could help the patient maintain, increase, and strengthen the achieved amelioration, even outside of the hospital environment. But of course I had no idea of how to do this. I had nevertheless learned that whatever benefit the patient could receive had to come from his bonds with at least another human being. It was something that neither Vico, nor Bleuler, nor Werner could teach me. It seemed to be difficult to establish a human bond with the schizophrenic, at a professional level; and Freud, whom I had read widely, did not seem much interested in the subject.

That is why, when I was "defrosted" and left Pilgrim State Hospital, I applied to become a candidate at the White Institute. I say "defrosted" because during the Second World War many people were "frozen"—

that is, compelled by the government to remain in their jobs for the duration of the war. After the war we became free to change jobs. I returned to New York as a practitioner and a student at the White Institute, where I knew it was possible to receive what I wanted—that interpersonal approach which I had already understood was so important for the schizophrenic. And at the White Institute were the people about whom I had heard so much, whose writings I had admired, and whom I was eager to meet in person. I refer to Harry Stack Sullivan, Clara Thompson, Erich Fromm and many others. At the White Institute I learned that one becomes a person by virtue of relations with other human beings and not of inborn instinctual drives.

I have not yet mentioned Frieda Fromm-Reichmann. It was from her I would learn those modalities that would maintain in a state of remission the patients whose temporary improvement I had seen at Pilgrim State Hospital. I learned from her that the countless ways, the infinite nuances with which people love or hate, help or hurt one another, can be observed better in the study of the schizophrenic disorder than in any other condition (Fromm-Reichmann, 1950). I have reported elsewhere (1968a) the memory of the last time I saw Frieda Fromm-Reichmann. In January 1957 she gave a speech to the graduating class of the William Alanson White Institute. I was one of the many people listening to her, and I was very much impressed by the many things she said about her experiences at Chestnut Lodge and in Palo Alto. But what has remained vivid in my mind was her mimicking of a female schizophrenic patient who always walked with a thumb extended and the other fingers flexed over the palm of her hand. Frieda did not interpret this gesture as others would have. For her, the extended thumb was not a phallic symbol, nor did it indicate penis envy. It meant, "I am one: alone, alone, alone!" What does the cry of loneliness mean to the schizophrenic patient, or, for that matter, to any human being? It means that one has been abandoned by the interpersonal world or is very much in need of intimacy with the interpersonal world. But the pain of aloneness and loneliness is felt inside, inside of what the lonely thumb stood for, the patient.

Fromm-Reichmann was indeed among the first to emphasize that the schizophrenic is not only alone in his world, but also lonely. His loneliness has a long and sad history. Contrary to what many psychiatrists used to believe, the patient is not happy with his withdrawal but is ready to resume interpersonal relations, provided that he finds a person who is capable of removing the suspiciousness and distrust that originated with the first interpersonal relations that made him follow a solitary path. In order to establish an atmosphere of trust, the therapist must treat the patient with kindness, understanding, and consideration, but not with condescending or smothering attitudes as if he were a baby. From Fromm-Reichmann I learned that a part of the patient has retained an adult life and would resent being treated as a baby. Fromm-Reichmann tried to explain to the patient that symptoms are ways of remodeling life experience in consequence of, or in accordance with, thwarted past or present interpersonal relations. She wanted the patient to become aware of the losses sustained early in life, but to become aware of them on a realistic level. That is, the patient must not distort or transform symbolically these losses but must accept the fact that they can never be made up and that he is nevertheless capable of becoming integrated with the interpersonal world. It will be easier for him to integrate when he recognizes his fear of closeness and, even more, his fear of hostility.

Not only from Frieda Fromm-Reichmann, but from the whole faculty of the White Institute, I learned that a characteristic unique to the human race—prolonged childhood with consequent extended dependency on adults and need of lasting and solid interpersonal relations—is the basis of the psychodynamics of schizophrenia. What occurs at any subsequent age is also relevant and may bring about the decisive turns of events that trigger the psychosis. The childhood situation, however, provides preparatory factors that have a funda- mental role inasmuch as they narrow the range of choices of life directions, thwart the possibility of compensation, determine basic orientations, and facilitate abnormal sequences of events.

In summary, my training at the White Institute taught me to study the world the child meets and the child's way of experiencing that world, especially in its interpersonal aspects. It also taught me what people can do to one another. I was thus able to attempt some formulations of the psychodynamics of schizophrenia. I was gradually filling the numerous gaps and doubts that my original observations at Pilgrim State Hospital had left in me. Soon, however, other doubts started to creep in, and I saw different types of gaps. By stressing the interpersonal, Sullivan and his followers did not intend to subtract the intrapsychic, but in practice many did so. They focused on the individual as if he were a *tabula rasa* molded passively by the inter- personal events of his life. Although by no stretch of the imagination should interpersonal theories be confused with behaviorism, they did stress the relation with the external world, and the response to that relation. The inner self was neglected, at least in theoretical conceptions.

It is true that inasmuch as the human being is strongly influenced by the environment, especially his interpersonal environment, we must acknowledge in him a fundamental state of *receptivity.* He cannot, however, be defined only in terms of a state of receptivity. Every human being, even in early childhood, has another basic function which we can call *integrative activity.* Just as the transactions with the world not only inform but transform the individual, with his integrative activity the individual transforms these transactions and in turn is informed and transformed by these transformations. *No* influence is received as a direct and immutable message. Multiple processes involving interpersonal and intrapsychic dimensions go back and forth.

I thought that I could find the clue to this integrative activity in cognition, an area of psychology regarded with great suspicion in the late forties and early fifties, when either behaviorism, instinctual Freudianism, or interpersonalism prevailed. I not only went back to Giambattista Vico and Heinz Werner, but also immersed myself in Hughlings Jackson, Kurt Goldstein, Jean Piaget, Susanne Langer, Kasanin, von Domarus, and the Russian Vygotsky. I repeat, this was during the late forties and early fifties. My approach aimed at finding structural forms for a psychodynamic content. This approach, which I called structural or psychostructural, was developed independently and along different lines from the studies of Lévi-Strauss, and preceded Chomsky's application of structuralism to other fields of inquiry. The topic on which I focused my research was thought disorder in schizophrenia. Needless to say, at that time most people did not know what I was talking about. A few, however, did. One of them was David Rioch, the brother of Janet Rioch, who in 1948 enthusiastically accepted my paper on the special logic of schizophrenia for publication in the journal *Psychiatry.* That paper opened to me the possibility of writing a book, and in 1955 the first edition of *Interpretation of Schizophrenia* appeared. In that book I tried to formulate a psychodynamics of schizophrenia, mostly based on my experience at the White Institute, and to integrate such formulations with my cognitive-structural studies.

It is impossible for me even to summarize here my work on schizophrenic cognition (1948, 1955, 1967, 1974b). I shall limit myself to a few points which either have relevance to the rest of this presentation or which can be understood by themselves.

What to the normal mind is only a state of similarity becomes for the schizophrenic mind a state of identity. In other words, two subjects are considered identical if they have a part, attribute, or characteristic in common. The patient focuses on that similarity and overlooks everything else. When the schizophrenic thinks in a typically schizophrenic way, he identifies not by virtue of identical subjects, as Aristotelian logic requires, but by virtue of identical predicates, that is, in accordance with the principle of von Domarus. As we shall see from the examples which follow, this need to identify subjects that should not be identified is extremely strong in the schizophrenic and has at least two motivations or purposes. The first is of a general character: that of recapturing some order or cognitive organization in the confused or fragmented schizophrenic world; the second, specific in each patient, is to believe as true and rational what he wishes to be true. An example I often cite is that of a patient who thought she was the Virgin Mary. Asked why, she replied, "I am a virgin; I am the Virgin Mary." The common predicate "being virgin" led to the identification of the two subjects, the Virgin Mary and the patient. Obviously the patient had the need to identify with the Virgin Mary, who was her ideal of perfection and to whom she felt close. At the same time she had the need to deny her feeling of unworthiness and inadequacy.

A red-haired 24-year-old woman in a postpartum schizophrenic psychosis developed an infection in one of her fingers. The terminal phalanx was swollen and red. She told the therapist a few times, "This finger is me." Pointing to the terminal phalanx, she said, "This is my red and rotten head." She did not mean that her finger was a representation of herself, but, in a way incomprehensible to us, really herself or an actual duplicate of herself. Another patient believed that the two men she loved in her life were actually the same person, although one lived in Mexico City and the other in New York. In fact both of them played the guitar and both of them loved her. By resorting to a primitive cognition which followed the principle of von Domarus, she could reaffirm the unity of the image of the man she wanted to love.

In Aristotelian logic, only like subjects are identified. The subjects are fixed; therefore, only a limited number of deductions are possible. In primary-process thinking the predicates lead to the identification. Since the predicates of the same subjects are numerous, the deduction reached by this type of thinking is not easy to predict. The choice of the predicate leading to the identification is psychodynamically determined by conscious or unconscious motivational trends.

This cognitive organization of the primary process is susceptible to different interpretations which actually refer to the same phenomena. We may, for instance, state that the primary process organizes classes or categories which differ from those of secondary-process thinking. In secondary-process thinking a class is a collection of objects to which a concept applies. For instance, Washington, Jefferson, Lincoln, and Roosevelt form a class to which the concept "President of the United States" applies. In paleologic or primary-process thinking a class is a collection of objects that have a predicate or part in common (for instance, the state of being virgin), and which, therefore, become identical or equivalent. The formulation of a primary (process) class is often an unconscious mechanism. Whereas the members of a secondary (process) class are recognized as being similar (and it is actually on their similarity that their classification is based), the members of a primary class are freely interchanged: for instance, the patient becomes the Virgin Mary.

Another characteristic of the paleologic organization is the change in the significance of words. They lose part of their connotation; they may not refer to a class anymore, but the verbalization, that is, the word as a phonetic entity, independent of its meaning, acquires prominence. Other primary-process mechanisms may take place after attention has been focused on verbalization. In many expressions of patients who think according to primary-process cognition, two or more objects or concepts are identified because they can be represented by the same word. The verbal symbol thus becomes the identifying predicate. This leads to what seem to be plays on words. For instance, a patient who was asked to define the word "life" started to define *Life* magazine. An Italian patient, whose name was Stella, thought she was a fallen star. Another patient thought she was black like the night. Her name was Laila, which means night in Hebrew.

Another primary-process mechanism, common to dreams and to schizophrenia, is the concretization of the concept. In schizophrenia concepts which cannot be endured by the patient as long as he uses them at an abstract level are translated into concrete representations. For instance, a patient had the delusion that his wife was poisoning his food. He had a gustatory hallucination which made him taste poison in his food. Treatment revealed that the patient was actually experiencing a general situation in which he felt his wife was "poisoning" his life. Another patient had an olfactory hallucination. He smelled a "bad odor" emanating from his body. He was concerned at an abstract level with his character. He felt he had a stinking personality. In many of my writings I have illustrated how many of the schizophrenic's delusions and ideas of reference can be interpreted from a formal or structural point of view as concretizations of concepts or as applications of the von Domarus principle. Other delusions derive from an altered relation between the connotation and the articulation of verbal symbols.

Still another problem which has interested me concerns hallucinations, which I feel cannot be studied exclusively from the point of view of their content. Let us assume that a patient hears a hallucinatory voice calling her a prostitute. We may say that the voice represents her guilt, externalized outside of herself. One may also say that the voice reproduces the early voice of her mother: "Joan, you act like a prostitute when you use so much lipstick. *I* know what you are going to be." This interpretation has a ring of truth, but the mark of schizophrenia here is not the abnormal relation with the mother. The abnormal relation with the mother could have revealed itself later as insecurity, excessive anxiety, or strong guilt feeling, but instead it manifested itself as an unusual mechanism, indeed, a schizophrenic symptom. Something that had been introjected became externalized again as a voice, a pseudo perception coming from the external world. It is thus necessary to study the mechanism not only in its content, but in its special cognitive schizophrenic form.

I cannot summarize all my work on hallucination, or how an emotionally loaded abstract concept is transformed into a perception and experienced as coming from the external world. We must remember, however, that projection also takes place in normal perception. Perception of an external stimulus, let us say of a visual stimulus, actually takes place internally in our cortical centers, around the calcarine fissure. However, the perception is projected outside and is experienced as a reproduction of the external environment. We are aware of the stimuli hitting us from outside, but we are not aware of the externalization of the perception into the outside world. This externalization coincides with what is known to us as a realistic status of the environment. Whether it is so, or whether some philosophers are correct in denying that perception reproduces external reality, is a problem that need not be discussed here. This externalization or projection, which occurs normally in perception, also occurs in hallucination. Inasmuch as the hallucination is experienced as a perception, the process of externalization is an implicit, necessary, concomitant characteristic.

An aspect of schizophrenic hallucinations which has always intrigued me is the difficulty in correcting the experience or the inability of the nontreated patient to recognize that the hallucination is a false perception having no foundation in reality. When the patient hallucinates, his thoughts regress to the perceptual level, and it is only with the means available at that level, that is, with his perceptions, that he evaluates what happens to him. In the first edition of *Interpretation of Schizophrenia* (1955) I stressed this inability of the patient to recognize the unrealistic nature of the hallucinations, unless, of course, he recovers. My further studies proved that I was wrong. The schizophrenic patient, during psychotherapy, can correct his hallucinatory experiences. As a matter of fact, with a special procedure I have devised and shall now describe, many patients are now able to recognize the unreality of the experience. In what follows I shall consider only auditory hallucinations, but the same procedures could be applied to other types of hallucination after the proper modifications have been made.

With the exception of patients who are at a very advanced stage of the illness or with whom no relatedness whatsoever can be reached, it is possible to recognize that the hallucinatory voices occur only in particular situations, that is, *when the patient expects to hear them.* For instance, a patient goes home after a day of work and expects the neighbors to talk about him. As soon as he expects to hear them, he hears them. In other words, he puts himself in what I have called *the listening attitude.*

If we have been able to establish not only contact but relatedness with the patient, he will be able, under our direction, to distinguish two stages: that of the listening attitude and that of the hallucinatory experience. At first he may protest vigorously and deny the existence of the two stages, but later he may make a little concession. He will say, "I happened to think that they would talk, and I proved to be right. They were really talking."

A few sessions later another step forward will be made. The patient will be able to recognize and to admit that there was a brief interval between the expectation of the voices and the hearing of the voices. He will still insist that this sequence is purely coincidental, but eventually he will see a connection between his putting himself into the listening attitude and his actually hearing. Then he will recognize that he puts himself into this attitude when he is in a particular situation or in a particular mood, for instance, a mood in which he is prone to perceive hostility, almost in the air. He has the feeling that everybody has a disparaging attitude toward him; he then finds corroboration for this attitude of others: he hears them making unpleasant remarks about him. At times he feels inadequate and worthless, but he does not sustain this feeling for more than a fraction of a second. The self-condemnation almost automatically induces him to put himself into the listening attitude, and then he hears other people condemning him.

When the patient is able to recognize the relation between the mood and putting himself into the listening attitude, a great step has been accomplished. He will not see himself any longer as a passive agent, as the victim of a strange phenomenon or of persecutors, but as somebody who still has a great deal to do with what he experiences. Moreover, if he catches himself in the listening attitude, he has not yet descended to or is not yet using abnormal or paleologic ways of thinking from which it will be difficult to escape. He is in the process of falling into the seductive trap of the world of psychosis, but he may still resist the seduction and remain in the world of reality. He will intercept the mechanism; he acquires the power to do so.

If an atmosphere of relatedness and understanding has been established, patients learn without too much difficulty to catch themselves in the act of putting themselves into the listening attitude, at the least disturbance, several times during the day. Although they recognize the phenomenon, they sometimes feel that it is almost an automatic mechanism which they cannot prevent. Eventually, however, they come to control it more and more. Even then, however, there is a tendency to resort again to the listening attitude and to the hallucinatory experiences in situations of stress. The therapist should never tire of explaining the mechanism to the patient again and again, even when such explanations seem redundant. They are seldom redundant, as the symptoms may reacquire an almost irresistible attraction.

Another major focus of my research has been on determining how special cognitive processes and conceptualizations of the patient alter the influences of the external world and bring about in the patient transformations which many authors have mistaken as faithful representations of reality. I shall explain what I mean in reference to two important issues: the concept of the "schizophrenogenic" mother and the future schizophrenic patient's self-image. These images of the mother and of the self are "inner objects" of crucial importance in any psychodynamic therapy.

The mother of the schizophrenic has been described as a malevolent creature deprived of maternal feeling. John Rosen (1953, 1962) spoke of her perverse sense of motherhood. She has been called a monstrous human being. At times it is indeed difficult not to make these negative appraisals because some examples, considered typical, seem to fit that image. Quite often, however, an unwarranted generalization is made. The mother of the patient is not a monster or an evil-doer, but a person who has been overcome by the difficulties of living. These difficulties have become enormous because of her unhappy marriage, but, most of all, because of her neurosis and the neurotic defenses she has built up in interacting with her children. Moreover, we must remember that the studies of these mothers were made immediately before the women's liberation era. In other words, they were made during a period in which the woman had to contend fully but most of the time tacitly with her newly emerged need to assert equality. She could not accept submission any longer, and yet she strove to fulfill her traditional role. These are not just social changes; they are factors that enter into the intimacy of family life and complicate the parental roles of both mothers and fathers.

In the last 18 years I have compiled some private statistics and, although personal biases cannot be excluded and the overall figures are too small to be of definite value, I have reached the tentative conclusion that only approximately 25 percent of the mothers of schizophrenics fit the image of the schizophrenogenic mother. I actually would be more inclined to say that only 20 percent correspond to this image, but I have included doubtful cases and conceded a maximum of 25 percent. Approximately 75 percent of the mothers do not fit this image. I have asked myself why these mothers have been portrayed in this intensely negative, judgmental way. Why do we find such descriptions in the writings of such different people as Sullivan (1953, 1962), Rosen (1953, 1962), Hill (1955), Lidz (1969), Laing (1967), and, I must reluctantly admit, Arieti (1955)? It would be too easy and certainly inaccurate to think that all of us had personal psychological needs to generalize to all cases what occurs in only a minority of typical cases.

Of course, one could say that I have erred in my calculations. The "monsters" would have succeeded once again in hiding from me their real nature and the subtle, intangible, invisible war and invisible hate that produced such visible effects. Frankly, I do not believe I have grown so insensitive, in many years of practicing psychoanalysis and psychotherapy, as to become less aware now than in the past of the invisible war and of the invisible hate.

Repeated observations have led me to different conclusions. Schizophrenics who are at a relatively advanced stage of psychoanalytically oriented therapy often describe their parents, especially the mother, in these negative terms, the terms used in the psychiatric literature. We therapists have believed what our patients have told us. Inasmuch as a considerable percentage of mothers have proved to be that way, it was easier for us to make an unwarranted generalization which included all the mothers of the schizophrenics. We have made a mistake reminiscent of the one made by Freud when he came to believe that neurotic patients had been assaulted sexually by their parents. Later Freud realized that what he had believed to be true was, in by far the majority of cases, only the product of the patient's fantasy. The comparison is not quite apt, because in possibly 25 percent of the cases the mothers of schizophrenic patients were really monstrous, and I do not know what percentage of mothers of nonschizophrenics are monstrous.

If my interpretation is correct, we must find out why many patients have transformed the image of the mother or of both parents into one which is much worse than the real one. In my opinion what happens in the majority of cases is the following: the mother has definite negative characteristics—excessive anxiety, hostility, or detachment. The future patient becomes particularly sensitized to these characteristics. He becomes aware only of them because they are the parts of mother that hurt and to which he responds deeply. He ignores the others. His use of primary-process cognition makes possible and perpetuates this partial awareness, this original part-object relationship, if one wants to use Melanie Klein's terminology. The patient who responds mainly to the negative parts of mother will try to make a whole out of these negative parts, and the resulting whole will be a monstrous transformation of mother. In later stages this negative image may attract negative aspects of other family members or of the family constellation, so that the mother's image will be intensified in its negative aspect. This vision of mother is to some degree understood by the mother, who responds to the child with more anxiety and hostility. A vicious circle is thus established, and it produces progressive and intense distortions and maladaptations. Two tendencies develop. One is the repression from consciousness of the reality of the mother-patient relationship, a task which cannot be easily achieved. The other tendency is to displace or project to some parts of the external world this state of affairs. However, this tendency too is not possible unless a psychosis occurs, and for the time being it remains only a potentiality. What I have said in relation to the mother could, in a smaller number of patients, be more appropriately said in reference to the father.

Similar remarks can be made for the self-image of the future patient. Those of us trained in the Sullivanian school have learned to conceive of the self as constituted of reflected appraisals. The patient thinks of himself what other people would think about him. Although Sullivan has stressed that the patient "selectively inattends" certain parts of these appraisals, and is mostly aware of that part called "the bad-me," this concept, as used by some people, only approximates the truth. What is not taken into account in this concept is that the self is not merely a passive reflection. The mechanism of the formation of the self is not merely absorption of what comes from the external world, nor can it be compared to the function of a mirror. If we want to use the metaphor of the mirror, we must specify that we mean an activated mirror which adds to the reflected images its own distortions, especially those distortions that at an early age are caused by primary-process cognition.

The young child does not respond equally to all appraisals and roles attributed to him. Those elements that hurt him more and, in some cases, please him more stand out and are integrated disproportionately. Thus the self, although related to the external appraisals, is not a reproduction of them but a grotesque representation. Moreover, the self is composed of all the defenses that are built to cope with these appraisals and their distortions. The more disturbed the environment, the more prominent is the role and lingering of primary-process cognition, which gives a special individualistic private form to inner images and other internal constructs (Arieti, 1948, 1974b). The grotesque representation of the self the patient retains would stupefy the parents if they were aware of it. According to my own private statistics, it would stupefy 80 percent of them, who never, consciously or unconsciously, wanted to inflict it on the children. This grotesque self-image is very painful and would become even more painful if the patient were to continue to be aware of it and were to continue to connect it with an increasing number of ramifications and implications. Fortunately, to a large extent, this image is repressed from awareness. The individual would not be able to bear it. During psychotherapy the patient becomes aware again of his own self-image, and consequently of his own despair and helplessness in confronting himself and others. A frequent outlet is to blame the parents for all this. The therapist and the patient often establish an alliance based on recrimination for what the parents have allegedly done in engendering this self-image and helplessness.

I have made an effort to change this prevailing therapeutic climate (Arieti, 1968b, 1974b). Obviously, the patient must, at some stage of treatment, become conscious of his helplessness and grotesque self-image. Contrary to what some psychiatrists believe, in most cases the patient is not aware of them. When he becomes aware, he must understand the roles played by his parents and family. However, he must also become aware of his own distortions, his own contributions to the build-

ing of his own private inner objects. This is not easy to do. Many
therapists, even today, are not able to help their patients in this matter,
which to me seems a crucial one. Why is it so difficult to help the
patient on this point?

At the stage of treatment in which the patient does not speak any
longer of persecutors but only of the malevolence of his parents, he
has made great improvement and in a technical sense is no longer
delusional. Distortions continue to exist, but they are not so easily
recognized or detected by the therapist as delusions are. Fortunately,
in every case some helpful clues can be found. In the newly developed
antiparental zeal, the patient goes on a campaign to distort not only
the past but also what the parent does and says *now*. Incidentally, this
tendency is present not only in schizophrenics, but also in some pre-
schizophrenics who never become full-fledged psychotics. By being
fixated in an antiparental frame of reference, they may not need to
become delusional and psychotic. To a much less unrealistic extent, this
tendency occurs in some neurotics, too. At times the antiparental campaign is enlarged to include parents-in-law and other people who have
a quasi-parental role.

The therapist has to help in many ways. First, he points out how
the patient distorts or exaggerates. For instance, a white lie is transformed into the worst mendacity, tactlessness into falsity or perversion.
These deformations are caused by the need to reproduce a pattern
established in childhood, a pattern that was the result not only of what
historically happened, but also of the patient's immaturity, ignorance,
and misperception. At times these deformations are easy to correct.
For instance, the mother of one patient told her, "Your mother-in-law
is sick." The patient interpreted her mother's words to mean: "With
your perverse qualities you have made your mother-in-law sick as you
once made me sick." On still another occasion the mother spoke about
the beautiful apartment that the patient's newly married younger sister
had just furnished. The patient, who, incidentally, was jealous of the
mother's attention to her sister, interpreted this remark as meaning,
"Your sister has much better taste than you."

Second, the patient must realize that the negative traits of parents
or other important people are not necessarily arrows or weapons used
purposely to hurt the patient. They are merely characteristics of these
people and should not be considered total qualities. For instance, in
the remarks of the patient's mother reported above, there might have
been some elements of hostility. Yet in every human relation and communication, in every social event, many dimensions and meanings exist,

not only in the so-called double-bind talk of the alleged schizophreno-genic mother. The patient, however, focuses on this negative trend or aspect and neglects all the other dimensions of the rich and multifaceted communication. The patient is unable to tolerate any ambivalence, any plurality of dimensions.

Third, and most important, the original parental introject must lose importance. The patient is an adult now; it is up to the patient to provide for himself or to search for himself what he once expected to get from his parents.

If space permitted, I would elaborate on my cognitive approach to psychoanalysis in general (1974a) and to depression in particular (1977b). Today cognition is studied not just as a form, but also as content; not as consisting of conflict-free areas, as Hartmann, Kris, and Lowenstein (1946) and Rapaport (1960) have considered it, but as the source of, or direct participant in, the conflict. Ideas are considered not as conflict-free, but as active participants or generators of conflicts (Arieti, 1974a).

Even the neo-Freudian schools have shown a reluctance to stress the importance of the idea as a major ingredient of the psyche, or as a source of conflict and pathology. There has been an almost prudish embarrassment in admitting that ideas count, a disinclination to investigate deeply what ideas do to men or what men do to ideas, so that they become disturbing factors. And yet I do not need to point out to anyone that in psychoanalytic therapy we deal with ideas constantly, and that almost all our exchanges with patients occur through ideas, and that it is through ideas that we bring about improvement or cure. A prevailing cultural anti-intellectualism has caused misapprehensions and distortions even in the field of psychoanalysis. When we stress the importance of ideas and systems of ideas, we do not minimize the importance of affective life, or of motivation, conscious or unconscious. On the contrary, we stress a fact very seldom acknowledged, namely, that at a human level most emotions would not exist without a cognitive substratum.

It was, however, not my stressing the importance of the idea that led me to become interested in the problem of creativity. I owe this interest again to my work with schizophrenics, and in particular to the apparently witty expressions I have heard from schizophrenic patients from the beginning of my psychiatric practice (Arieti, 1950). To be exact, these witty expressions are witty for us, not for the patient, who uses them in complete seriousness. A patient whom I examined at Pilgrim State Hospital during the Second World War told me that next time the Japanese attacked the Americans, it would be at Diamond Harbor or Gold Harbor. When she was asked why, she replied, "The first time, they attacked at Pearl Harbor; now they will attack at Diamond or at Sapphire Harbor." "Do you think that the Japanese attacked Pearl Harbor because of its name?" I asked. "No, no," she replied. "It was a happy coincidence." Note the inappropriateness of the adjective "happy." It was a happy coincidence for her because she could thereby prove the alleged validity of her primary-process thinking.

A patient whom I examined many years ago had the habit of oiling her body. Asked why she did so, she replied, "The human body is a machine and has to be lubricated." The word "machine," applied in a figurative sense to the human body, had led to the identification with man-made machines. The patient meant literally what she said. Her delusional remark is witty only for us. In this case, too, we, not the patient, create the joke, because we recognize illogicality in her apparent logicality.

Another patient complained that there were two initials on an office door at her place of employment that referred to her. They were "O.B.," and she thought they meant she was an "Old Bag." Although she worked in that office, she conveniently overlooked that they stood for "Ordering and Billing." Another patient, whom I discussed in supervision, thought he was Jesus Christ. When asked why, he said, "Well, I have had so much Carnation milk that now I am reincarnated."

These are examples of the primary process catching similarities, which I discussed at the beginning of this paper; but they are similarities not controlled by the secondary process. My subsequent studies of wit and the comic disclosed that the person who is creative in these fields catches these similarities in accordance with the von Domarus principle. He must also rely on the processes mentioned earlier in this paper, namely, semantic alteration (or partial loss of connotation) and increased value of the verbalization (or formal pregnancy). In creativity these primitive processes are coordinated with those of the secondary process to form what I call the tertiary process.

I see the creative or tertiary process as a harmonic combination of primary- and secondary-process mechanisms. In accordance with special structures and forms that I have described in my book *Creativity: The Magic Synthesis* (1976), the tertiary process blends the rational and the irrational. Instead of rejecting the primitive (or whatever is archaic, obsolete, or off the beaten path), the creative mind integrates it with normal logical processes in what seems a "magic" synthesis from which the new, the unexpected, and the desirable emerge.

In my book I have discussed several fields of creativity: science, religion, philosophy, mysticism, and general systems theory. Particularly close to my heart is the field of poetry, in which I have also illustrated the semantic alterations and the increased value of verbalization as they come from the primary process and become coordinated with the secondary process. The primary-process quality of catching similarities in accordance with the von Domarus principle reveals itself especially in the poetic metaphor. Often the poet has as great a capacity for imagery as does the dreamer, or he has a capacity for "orgies of identification" similar to that of the schizophrenic. He is able, however, to use these images in unpredictable syntheses, which become works of art. For instance, Victor Hugo, in his poems, compares the stars, in multiple and, to the average person, inconceivable ways: to diamonds, golden clouds, golden pebbles, lamps, lighted temples, flowers of eternal summer, silvery lilies, eyes of the night, vague eyes of the twilight, embers of the sky, holes in a huge ceiling, bees which fly in the sky, drops of Adam's blood, and even to the colored spots on the tail of the peacock.

The successful metaphor, even when it seems to subtract from reality, adds to our understanding and confers esthetic value. When the poet says A is like B, where nobody else would be able to see that similarity, he transports us into a universe where real and unreal unite and gives us a vision of unsuspected depths and dimensions. When Shakespeare, in *Macbeth,* writes:

> *...Out, out, brief candle*
> *Life's but a walking shadow, a poor player*
> *That struts and frets his hour upon the stage,*
> *And then is heard no more; it is a tale*
> *Told by an idiot, full of sound and fury,*
> *Signifying nothing...*

we perceive a greater, even if dubious, understanding. The poet purports to give us a series of definitions of life. Were we to remain in the realm of our daily reality, we could insist that life is not a candle, is not a walking shadow, is not a poor player, is not a tale told by an idiot. But our realism is suspended. Although these definitions of life are not those given in the dictionary or in a textbook of biology, we sense that we are getting closer to touching a special truth that only the metaphor can offer us. The metaphor seems to transport us closer to a world of absolute understanding that is more real than reality. At the same time, we are conscious that these words are pronounced by Macbeth, the hero of evil—certainly not a man whom we should listen to as a master of life. Is he right? Is he wrong? Is this vision of life determined by a life of crime? There are no sure answers to these questions.

I am aware that, especially in the field of creativity, I have given a very inadequate sample of what I have reported in various writings. Let me conclude, however, by formulating in a few words the message that I have tried to convey in shifting from schizophrenia to creativity.

A psychiatrist who does not want to be only a dispenser of drugs cannot avoid adventuring beyond the field of psychiatry. The blending of ideas and feelings, of truth and illusion, of what is original in a bizarre way and what is a precursor of creativity, of the fantasy that leads to delusion and the one that leads to art, of the conflict that causes terrible pain and the one that leads to growth, is something that cannot be visualized in the restricted framework of a daily, purely clinical work. But when the psychiatrist goes beyond psychiatry, he must do so as a psychiatrist, that is, by making good use of that immense patrimony of knowledge and feeling with which psychiatry has provided him.

REFERENCES

Arieti, S. (1948), Special logic of schizophrenic and other types of autistic thought. *Psychiatry,* 11:325–338.

————— (1950), New views on the psychology and psychopathology of wit and of the comic. *Psychiatry,* 13:43–62.

————— (1955), *Interpretation of Schizophrenia.* New York: Brunner.

————— (1967), *The Intrapsychic Self: Feeling, Cognition and Creativity in Health and Mental Illness.* New York: Basic Books.

————— (1968a), Some memories and personal views. *Contemp. Psychoanal.,* 5:85–89.

————— (1968b), The psychodynamics of schizophrenia: A reconsideration. *Amer. J. Psychother.* 22:366–381.

————— (1974a), The cognitive-volitional school. In: *American Handbook of Psychiatry,* 2nd ed., 1:877–903. New York: Basic Books.

————— (1974b), *Interpretation of Schizophrenia,* rev. ed. New York: Basic Books.

————— (1976), *Creativity: The Magic Synthesis.* New York: Basic Books.

————— (1977a), The parents of the schizophrenic patient: A reconsideration. *J. Amer. Acad. Psychoanal.,* 5:347–358.

————— (1977b), Psychotherapy of severe depression. *Amer. J. Psychiat.* 134:864–868.

Hartmann, H., Kris, E., & Lowenstein, R.M. (1946), Comments on the formation of psychic structure. *The Psychoanalytic Study of the Child,* 2:11–38. New York: International Universities Press.

Hill, L.B. (1955), *Psychotherapeutic Intervention in Schizophrenia.* Chicago: University of Chicago Press.

Fromm-Reichmann, F. (1950), *Principles of Intensive Psychotherapy.* Chicago: University of Chicago Press.

Laing, R.D. (1967), *The politics of Experience.* New York: Pantheon Books.

Lidz, T. (1969), The influence of family studies in the treatment of schizophrenia. *Psychiatry,* 32:237–251.

Rapaport, D. (1960), *The Structure of Psychoanalytic Theory* [*Psychological Issues,* Vol. 2, No. 2]. New York: International Universities Press.

Rosen, J. (1953), *Direct Analysis. Selected Papers.* New York: Grune & Stratton.

Rosen, J.N. (1962), *Direct Psychoanalytic Psychiatry.* New York: Grune & Stratton.

Sullivan, H.S. (1953), *Conceptions of Modern Psychiatry.* New York: Norton.

Sullivan, H.S. (1962), *Schizophrenia As a Human Process.* New York: Norton.

3

FROM EGO PSYCHOLOGY TO A PSYCHOLOGY OF SELF

GERARD CHRZANOWSKI, M.D.

THE ADVENT OF EGO PSYCHOLOGY

EGO PSYCHOLOGY has been widely hailed as the dawn of a psychoanalytic renaissance—a creative period between the old and the new view of *homo psychoanalyticus*. Freud's theoretical shift from his initial topographic to a structural model, as outlined in "The Ego and the Id" (1923), represents an effort to broaden the clinical scope of psychoanalysis. The earlier model with its linear progression from unconscious to preconscious to conscious thoughts was transcended by a construct of agencies of the human mind. Nevertheless, the underlying metapsychological assumptions of the topographic theory did not change with the emergence of the structural scheme. It should also be kept in mind that the constructs of ego, id, and superego were concretized, dogmatized, and given a quasi-anatomical status.

A more specific formulation of ego psychology emerged largely based on the work of Heinz Hartmann, the contributions of Anna Freud, and the formulations of Erik Erikson. David Rapaport was an ardent advocate of the newer point of view. The ego was accorded a measure of autonomy. Reality factors, social, cultural, interpersonal, and transactional considerations paved the way for a rapprochement between inner conflict and the network of human relations that are tributary to difficulties in living. Unfortunately, ego psychology failed to emancipate itself from its metapsychological moorings and its mechanistic model of human nature, thus perpetuating a clinical cul de sac.

EMERGENCE OF A PSYCHOLOGY OF SELF

In the wake of ego psychology a new interest in a psychology of self made its appearance. The British object-relations school, as represented by Fairbairn, Guntrip, and Winnicott, formulated a synthesis between an endopsychic and interpersonal construct of the self. Laing (1962) wrote a pioneering book called *The Divided Self* wherein the self transcends the structure of an ego. Among the so-called neo-Freudians the concept of self takes on clinical significance. Fromm (1947) uses the term "self" freely as a unique, individual manifestation. Horney (1937) speaks of an "inauthentic" as well as of an "idealized self." Sullivan (1953) conceived of the self as the content of consciousness and as the part of the personality central to the awareness of anxiety. To Sullivan the self is never an entity, but rather a dynamic process that depends on the interpersonal situation in which it reveals itself. Sullivan's "self" is an action-bound system that defies concretization.

Among classical psychoanalysts the term "self" has found its way into the thinking of many major theoreticians. From Hartmann to Edith Jacobson to Kohut, Kernberg, and others, the term is being used with increasing frequency.

CLASSICAL DEFINITION OF THE SELF

Hartmann (1958) uses the term "self" in a descriptive way, that is, as a reference to one's body, one's physical, psychic self, or similar designations. Edith Jacobson in *The Self and the Object World* (1964) makes a sharp distinction between self, self-representation, and the system ego. According to her, the system ego is intimately connected with the discovery of the object world and the increasing distinction between ego, on the one hand, and one's own physical and mental self, on the other hand. Initially, ill-defined images of the love objects combine with images of the bodily and psychic self. Gradually these vague images emerge as consistent and relatively realistic endopsychic representations of the object world and of the self.

Kohut in *The Analysis of the Self* (1971) refers to the self as a psychoanalytic abstraction pertaining to the content of the mental apparatus. To Kohut, the self is not an agency of the mind, but rather a structure of the mind. Kohut considers the self as a psychic structure to be cathected with instinctual energy as well as a structure of the mind with continuity in time. In his scheme the self is a content of the mental apparatus, but not one of its constituents.

In his most recent book, *The Restoration of the Self* (1977), Kohut re-examines a number of established theoretical concepts in order to define what it is that leads to the cure of self pathology. He now speaks of the necessity of two approaches—that is, a psychology in which the self is seen as the center of the psychological universe, and a psychology in which the self is seen as a content of the mental apparatus. In my judgment this dualism constitutes the maintenance of a meta-psychological dogma and precludes the possibility of a genuinely open-ended system designed to increase the scope of clinical observation. Kohut rejects the notion of drive fixation associated with corresponding developmental arrest of the ego as a basically valid approach to self pathology. He presents poignant arguments against traditional classical formulations only to bow in the end to a psychoanalytic see. One is reminded of Galileo who was forced by religious authorities to nod his head to scientific misconceptions of his time that ran counter to his far-reaching new discoveries. I do not consider Kohut to be another Galileo. My reference is to his compulsion to "add a new dimension to the old principle." In doing so Kohut recommends that a psychology of the self be added to ego psychology, the psychology of a structural model of the mind, and the psychology of the drives.

Kohut's new psychology of self is unduly burdened by an excessive amount of dead weight. He does not stand behind his own convictions. A key consideration here is the classical point of view that looks at experience as a veneer covering a deeper level of psychological functioning.

CRITICAL EVALUATION OF THE CLASSICAL POINT OF VIEW

I fail to see how a psychology of self can coexist with the abstractions of id, ego, and superego as the structural underpinning of all experience. There is a major distinction between Kohut's formulation of a psychology of the self and the psychology of self advocated in this paper and in some of my previous writings. The difference will be spelled out in some detail later. At this point I only wish to reiterate that classical theoreticians look at the self as a potential surface phenomenon, that is, as a thin social or interpersonal overlay that conceals the inherent basic human stuff. Classical analysts accord id, ego, and superego an excessively concrete status in contrast to the self, which is not considered to be an integral part of the psychic apparatus. The classical self is depicted as a poor relation of the ego which is recognized as a most respectable part of the psychic establishment.

EGO PSYCHOLOGY AND ITS DERIVATIVES

It has become increasingly clear in recent years that ego psychology is old wine in a new bottle. The hope that ego psychology would bring psychoanalytic metapsychology in tune with social, cultural, and inter-personal phenomena has not been fulfilled. Ego psychology is solidly tied to the concretization of a psychic apparatus. Ego, id, and superego are given preference as elementary mental structures in contrast to the self which is considered to be an auxiliary, descriptive term pointing to the person as a subject (Jacobson, 1964). The ego-psychological self remains an experience-distant abstraction defying direct clinical ob-servation.

Theoretical modifications have also not sufficiently changed formal modalities of analysis pertaining to many ritualized aspects of analytic procedure (frequency of sessions, exclusive use of free association, interpreting according to a stereotyped system and so forth). Further-more, writers such as Fromm (1970), and Lacan (1969), each from a somewhat different perspective, take issue with the adaptational and conforming goals of ego psychology. Both men, consider ego psychology as a mechanistic formula for dehumanizing people.

In *The Crisis of Psychoanalysis* (Fawcett Premier, 1970) Fromm accuses ego psychology of dispensing with the core of Freud's system, i.e., the "science of the irrational." According to Fromm the ego psy-chological revision puts all the emphasis on the rational aspects of adaptation. Fromm states: "The knowledge and brilliance of the ego psychologists was apparently a great gift for a movement that had lost its 'cause', had neglected the productive development of 'id psychology', had looked for theoretical recognition, and did not want to be disturbed by its uncritical pursuit of dated ideas and therapeutic practices."

Lacan in *Ecrits: A Selection* (W.W. Norton, 1977, translated by Alan Sheridan) makes some pithy comments about ego psychology. In Chapter IV entitled The Freudian Thing under the heading "Inter-lude" he ridicules the idea of viewing the ego as a thing that is autono-mous. He refers to such a concept as "the latest fetish introduced into the holy of holies of a practice that derives its authority from the superior-ity of the superiors." Lacan goes on to say, "From thirty-five years of cohabitation with the ego under the roof of the second Freudian topography, including ten years of a stormier liaison, regularized at last through the good offices of Miss Anna Freud in a marriage whose social credit has been on the up and up ever since, to the point that I am assured that it will soon request the blessing of the church, in short, from the most sustained work of psychoanalysts, you will draw nothing more than this drawer."

The situation is quite different with other ego psychologies. Fairbairn (1954), Guntrip (1969) Winnicott (1965), Khan (1974), and others have made valuable contributions by emancipating themselves from a considerable body of Freudian metapsychology. So has Sullivan (1953) to a major degree. Nevertheless, the object-relations theorists must still rely on the concept "objects" rather than "people." Fairbairn (1954) still speaks of libido as if it were a heat sensor when he states: "Libido is essentially object seeking." Winnicott, Guntrip, Khan, and others have come a long way in describing an ego that bears little resemblance to the Freudian model of the psyche. Although Sullivan no longer uses the term "ego" he still has difficulty in arriving at a useful definition of "self." He is still burdened by his adherence to the principle of energy transformation as an explanatory phenomenon in spite of his emphatic rejection of psychic energy.

SULLIVAN'S PSYCHOLOGY OF SELF

Sullivan (1964) indubitably gave much thought to the genesis of the self and its dynamic transactions in interpersonal situations. His basic model centers on the organizations of experience; he stays relatively clear of psychic structures and avoids an adherence to closed systems. Nevertheless, his self is at the mercy of anxiety and lacks a continuity in its own right.

Sullivan's construct of self is a system forever caught in operational anonymity. To a large degree, self-esteem is the major characteristic commodity that pertains to the self. A person's basic level of self-esteem is inculcated early in life and is a cross to be carried from then on. According to Sullivan, it is doubtful that the core level of self-esteem can be raised much beyond the developmental epoch of pre-adolescence. At that time, the basic, underlying self-image is fairly well engraved. This does not mean that the future is totally bleak if the self-esteem has not been shored up at that level. Favorable changes, however, will be much more difficult to achieve, and they will not be as solidly anchored as they are in people who inherently think more highly of themselves.

Sullivan's major contribution consists in viewing the self as rooted in a network of relatedness to one's fellow human beings. He has pioneered the model of an ecosystem, an interpenetrating, transactional unit linking the self with its experiential *modus vivendi*. Sullivan's self exists exclusively in the process of defining itself by interacting with another human being. A self removed from its essential interpersonal setting reflects a morbid specimen since it is deprived of its natural habitat.

Sullivan denounces the notion of a static, fixed self as an illusion. He rejects the idea of an atomistic construct of the self and refuses to look at the self as a God-given, indivisible core of man.

To Sullivan a self cannot exist by itself since it invariably requires another self to come to the fore. Accordingly, he considers the concept of a real self to be misleading. Up to this point Sullivan's formulation of self stands on sound epistemological foundations. His reasoning loses some of its clarity when he opposes individual personality. After all, experience, the foundation of Sullivan's self, is a highly individual phenomenon. It is also doubtful that the evolution and maintenance of self and its concomitant self-esteem depend primarily on the approval of significant others and the relative freedom from the occurrence of anxiety.

FOUNDATION FOR A PSYCHOLOGY OF SELF

To my way of thinking, self, ego, personality, identity, intimacy—to mention just a few—are verbal tools fashioned for the task of exploring vaguely or inaccurately charted human territory. Each term is a construct that represents a part of a larger configuration. It is not of major importance which term we prefer as long as we recognize the heuristic, open-ended nature of each term. (See my chapters on "The Therapeutic Process" and "The Emergence of an Interpersonal Self" in *Interpersonal Approach to Psychoanalysis* [1977]).

With the advent of psychoanalysis, initially open-ended descriptive terms were increasingly endorsed with a pseudoscientific authority. This "validation" led to a concretization and reification of the terms. Accordingly, each term assumed a specific meaning and became associated with psychoanalytic structure, process, rituals, and mystique. In other words, a verbal, theoretical scaffolding was turned into dogma. The principle runs counter to the scientific use of verbal tools such as self, ego, and unconscious, to serve as temporary devices until more facts about a particular gap in knowledge have been accumulated.

My personal preference for the term "self" is based on the fact that terms such as "ego," "personality," "identity," and others have assumed a distinctly biased meaning while the construct "self" has a potentially more open-ended stance. An additional concern pertaining to the use of deterministic verbal tools is their coercive impact on our mental processes and observations.

It should be evident from the material presented so far that a psychology of self must stand on its own merit. There is no room for a self with a Janus head, that is, a single head with two faces pointing in opposite directions. A psychology of self can open the door to novel psychological territory only if it transcends the pitfalls of ego psychology, the structural model of agencies of the mind, and the psychology of the drives. Such a psychology also needs to rise above any concretization of a self. By the same token it must deal with individuality and remove itself from energic considerations.

One major consideration in beginning to forge a psychology of self is to gain valid information pertaining to the ways and means of maintaining as well as enhancing self-esteem.

Clinical Illustration of Self-Esteem

A brief clinical vignette will illustrate my point. The case is that of a young professional woman of superior intellectual endowment. Her family was unable to cope with her free-wheeling formative years. The parents were deeply troubled people who found a kind of tranquillity in applying themselves to compulsive, routinized work. A younger sibling was pressed into the same mold and grew up in the parental image, repeating their life, social, and performance patterns.

The patient was an outstanding student until she entered college where she acted out sexually, scholastically, and socially. Her post-graduate work was stormy, poorly organized, and led to a number of difficulties. She obtained a professional position in a highly prestigious setting, but managed to get fired from her job because of persistent absence and an inability to get her work done in spite of her acknowledged high level of competence. The patient went through several jobs, often working with distinction, but also with increasing unreliability.

She suffered two severe psychotic episodes requiring hospitalization of medium duration. Both times her overt psychosis manifested itself while she was in analytic therapy. The episodes were characterized by a complete break with reality, overt paranoid ideation, morbid sexual fantasies, and a wide range of major psychopathology.

This woman's postpsychotic adjustment was very good. Her case serves as an illustration of those patients who emerge stronger and humanly more intact from the ordeal. There were indications that her self-esteem rose after she overcame her collapse and temporary disintegration. Gradually many things fell in line for the patient, and she was able to organize her personal and professional life with increasing satisfaction. Although she evidenced fleeting, shaky moments of instability, her basic stability was of a high order.

Two problems remained: her excessive sensitivity to the disturbances of others and her profound difficulty in maintaining her own boundaries in that respect, and her persistent unreliability about time and routine work requirements. She was highly appreciated at work and treated with respect and consideration. Nevertheless, her excessive absenteeism (staying in bed and doing nothing) and lack of follow-through once more backed her into a corner where she had to show up and complete assignments or be dismissed. During this particular crisis, the patient reported a series of highly significant dreams. In one key dream she and her father (a man who undermined her self-esteem particularly during her juvenile and preadolescent period) were working on the same job. It was then announced that in order to stay on the job, she had to obtain a divorce from her father (both parents are living and active in their own right). After this dream, which greatly startled her, she had a nightmare reminiscent of her last psychotic episode. The dream was about a girl who had a nervous breakdown on the job and had to leave, followed by bizarre events involving an "eye bank" and eyes floating around.

One may interpret her dreams in many ways, with the traditional oedipal theme coming to mind first. In that respect it did not matter whether she had to separate from her actual father or from a father surrogate (the analyst). In the therapeutic situation it was suggested to her that she ask herself precisely what the metaphor of divorcing her father meant to her. In the meantime, a working hypothesis was pursued whereby the divorce from the father, whatever its particular significance may have been, was intimately tied to her self-esteem. The question then arose as to what the foundations of her self-esteem were and what affected it most directly in the here and now. This illustrates the difficulty of working with a global concept like self-esteem, its genesis and its ongoing maintenance operations.

Healthy Self-Esteem

Low self-esteem, like insecurity, is a ubiquitous characteristic. Probably the majority of mankind suffers from it in one form or another. But there is considerable difficulty in quantifying as well as qualifying feelings of worthlessness and deciding at which level they become morbid manifestations.

My clinical observations have demonstrated to me the highly individualized nature of a person's self-esteem. We are not dealing primarily with an approval-seeking self that begins to develop and grow when it encounters acceptance. Neither does it suffice to overcome powerful early life propaganda about being of a bad seed or something of that order. What is required is to be in touch with one's particular liabilities as well as one's distinctly personal assets. No substitute for it exists.

The above illustration shows that some people grow up with a persistent Achilles heel, i.e., a vulnerable, thinly covered area of low self-esteem. This clinical reality can be more effectively dealt with by ascribing to the self a personalized form and shape rather than treating it as an amorphous phenomenon.

In my definition, the self has three dimensions. They consist of: (1) *native endowment* (temperament, intellectual capacity, constitutional factors): (2) *experiential or epigenetic characteristics* (early plus longitudinal interpersonal integrations); and (3) *here-and-now transactions* (present-day phenomena under conditions that prevail, including transference-countertransference phenomena). *Self-esteem* is a highly individualized, personally rooted system that includes all three dimensions of the self. It calls for a clarification of one's native endowment, an appreciation of lifelong integrational patterns, and some understanding of here-and-now transactions in terms of undermining or slowing up the emergence of an interpersonal self.

Role of the Therapist

It is my contention that the emergence of a psychology of self promotes a sounder platform for therapeutic explorations. We are no longer burdened by confronting a generalized other person by a generalized self. Contrary to Sullivan, individuality comes into the picture by focusing explicitly on the way in which personal experiences are communicated by the patient and responded to in a personal way by the analyst. By definition, a participant observer does not assume a strictly neutral stance. Nevertheless, he functions more in the role of instrument than as his particular interpersonal self. (Much of this trans-actional phenomenon is still referred to by most analysts, including myself, as the transference-countertransference phenomenon even though it no longer refers to its original metapsychological terminology, i.e., an imprinted, habitual response system.)

Practically speaking, we are still compelled to use in our thinking verbal tools that are not in keeping with our ideology. For instance, I no longer have a need to think in terms of a weak or strong ego as a constitutional prognostic quantity. It no longer guides me in my therapeutic expectations. On the other hand, I still find myself think-ing of an observing ego. Intellectually, I have no use for the notion that a corner of my ego peeks at the rest of my ego while I am behaving irrationally. Neither can I really accept the concept of splitting of the ego even though I still use the term occasionally. The same holds true for the primary and secondary processes which I basically reject as a carry-over of the initial topographic layer concept. All these metaphors are still in my head and occasionally interfere with an unencumbered capacity to observe and conceptualize clinical data.

Another Clinical Illustration

The above-mentioned concept may be further elaborated by an-other illustration. I still do not quite know how I got there, but I have come to be some sort of authority on the syndrome of hypo-chondriasis. The term refers to the morbid preoccupation with ill health and represents a highly complex phenomenon. For the purpose of my presentation, it will suffice to focus on only one particular aspect, that is, the collusive misuse of hpyochondriacal language.

In certain familial and societal settings, we find a distinct in-junction against language of a personal nature. The participants in the communication rely predominantly on linguistic concretization. Organ language is a safe territory in bypassing individualized messages. Reference to symptoms of the body provide an emotionally accessible channel for many personally troublesome feelings. In other words, symbolic language (something is physically and also economically wrong with me) obscures both the awareness and the transmission of personal, distressing experiences of a nonphysical nature. Accordingly, many hypochondriacal people have no experience in making their feelings known to themselves and others. They frequently rely on an interpersonal repertory that is characterized by a linguistic impoverishment.

I saw a young married woman who had a number of children. She was the hypochondriacal daughter of a hypochondriacal mother. Her tolerance for her mother's morbid preoccupation with physical illness was low, and she could not control her own florid imagination about her own as well as her children's state of ill health, or, rather, the never-ending anxiety about it. The patient lived in a state of constant apprehension that an illness of a fatal nature had befallen her, her children, or others about whom she cared deeply. Her fear of malignancies ranging from leukemia to every imaginable form of cancer tortured her morning, noon, and night.

Much of our early work centered on her symptoms, on the time and circumstances when they first occurred, and on the purpose they may have served, particularly on possible areas of displacement. Frequent reference was made to her relationship with her mother and some overlapping patterns that pertained to her husband. It required a considerable amount of time to transcend her compulsive hypochondriacal and phobic preoccupations. Gradually, slowly, a minimum of personal information trickled through the maze of somatic metaphors. A few personal fantasies with a masochistic quality came to the fore although most of her communications were still fixated on a morbid level.

Her presentations had a poignant quality to them, and I detected a mild note of morbid fascination with her symptoms on my part. The thought occurred to me when I realized that I neither got bored nor irritated with her endless, alarming dramatizations. Finally I caught on to the fact that the patient's vivid imagination indicated a genuine gift on her part as a storyteller. I realized that she was a highly talented individual who never had allowed herself to give vent to her creative side. It was a genuine pleasure to listen to her stories about people, her personal observations, and the scope of her emotional range in discussing other people's predicaments. I told the patient my impressions about her native gift, which she first tried to brush off, but later she came to understand the basis for my opinion.

A series of highly dramatic events took place in this woman's life which are not relevant to my illustration of the hypochondriacal syndrome and certain technical considerations connected with it. What emerged with increasing clarity, however, was the remarkable widening of the patient's communicative channels. We fruitfully explored significant aspects of the transference-countertransference continuum. A wealth of intimate thoughts on the patient's part pertaining to her hopes, wishes, and fears emerged with considerable clarity. Although there were still minor flurries of hypochondriacal preoccupation, they no longer caused much commotion. The analysis came to a satisfactory termination, and the presenting symptom of hypochondriasis receded to a non-morbid level.

It is my conviction that the recognition of her finely tuned mind, her creative imagination, and her genuine gift as a storyteller were significant therapeutic observations. She had not been in touch with the range of her imaginative capacities and had concentrated exclusively on the somatic channel to give vent to her feelings. Many paranoid, frustrated, bitter, and unhappy feelings had to be worked through before she could reveal the scope of her constructive sensitivities. The revelation that the patient had managed to hold the analyst's attention with basically unproductive material proved to be helpful. It was possible to demonstrate to the patient that her repetitive somatic and phobic complaints ordinarily would evoke somnolent detachment or selective inattention.

SUMMARY

In my presentation I have attempted to outline a shift from the paradigm of ego psychology to an emerging psychology of self. It has been pointed out that ego psychology represents a facade for a set of metapsychological assumptions that have not stood the test of time. Early hopes of freeing ego psychology from its ideational thralldom and placing it on an empirical platform of its own have not materialized.

In a similar vein, the emerging psychology of self has not emancipated itself from old metapsychological chains. Powerful barriers associated with the reification of psychoanalytic dogma stand in the way. It has been illustrated how classical analysts give the self an auxiliary position while they elevate the abstract of the ego to a quasi-biological agency of the mind. My objection to this formulation is the classical tendency to view the self as a social veneer that covers the inner workings of the human psyche.

I have also addressed myself to the psychology of the self most recently advocated by Heinz Kohut. In my judgment he creates a false Janus head by adding a new dimension to an old principle. I doubt that the self can wear two faces looking in opposite directions. My main criticism of Kohut's point of view is his inability to divorce himself from traditional analytical assumptions and start in a fresh direction.

Reference has been made to the contributions of the object-relations school and to Sullivan's psychology of self.

My own recommendation is to build the foundations for a psychology of self. In doing so it seems necessary to liberate the self from its instrumental and anonymous position. Care should be taken not to concretize the self, but rather to deal with it as an open-ended system.

I have expressed the opinion here and elsewhere that psychoanalytic terminology is an important observational and communicative instrumentality. The language of psychoanalysis has been dualistic. One part is rooted in a humanistic philosophy while the other pertains to a neurophysiological model. Like the mind-body problem this dualism has made far reaching, often unrecognized inroads into psychoanalytic ideology. A psychology of self requires a language of its own that does not hark back to the reification of unsupported and often disproven assumptions. It needs to transcend analytical mythology and dogma in order to gain a better understanding of people's self-appraisal. A major task in this respect is to gather clinically valid data about the foundations and maintenance of a healthy self-esteem.

REFERENCES

Arlow, Jacob A.; Edward, Joseph D.; Peterfreund, Emanuel; Holt, Robert R. "Symposium on The Ego and the Id After Fifty Years" The Psychoanalytic Quarterly, Vol. 44, No. 4, 1975, pp. 509–576.

Blanck, G. and Blanck, R. (1974), *Ego-Psychology*. New York: Columbia University Press.

Chrzanowski, G. (1967), The independent roots of ego psychology and their therapeutic implications. In: *Science and Psychoanalysis,* Vol. XI, ed. J. Masserman. New York: Grune & Stratton.

―――― (1971), The changing language of self. *Contemp. Psychoanal.,* 7: 190–199.

―――― (1973a), Implications of interpersonal theory. In: *Interpersonal Explorations in Psychoanalysis,* ed. E. Witenberg. New York: Basic Books.

―――― (1973b), The rational id and the irrational ego. *J. Amer. Acad. Psychoanal.,* 1:231–241.

―――― (1974), Neurasthenia and hypochondriasis. In: *American Handbook of Psychiatry,* 2nd ed., ed. S. Arieti. New York: Basic Books.

―――― (1977), *Interpersonal Approach to Psychoanalysis: Contemporary*

View of Harry Stack Sullivan. New York: Gardner Press.

———— (1976), The psychoanalytic work of Erich Fromm, Karen Horney and Harry Stack Sullivan. In: *Psychology of the Twentieth Century,* Vols. II & III. Zurich: Kindler Verlag.

Fairbairn, W.R.D. (1954), *An Object-Relations Theory of Personality.* New York: Basic Books.

Fromm, E. (1970), *The Crisis of Psychoanalysis,* Greenwich, Conn.: Fawcett.

Freud, S. (1923), The ego and the id. *Standard Edition,* 19:3–59. London: Hogarth Press, 1961.

Guntrip, H. (1969), *Schizoid Phenomena, Object Relations and the Self.* New York: International Universities Press.

Hartmann, H. (1958), *Ego Psychology and the Problem of Adaptation.* New York: International Universities Press.

Havens, L.L. (1973), *Approaches to the Mind.* Boston: Little, Brown.

Horney, K. (1937), *The Neurotic Personality of our Time,* W.W. Norton & Co., New York.

Jacobson, E. (1964), *The Self and the Object World.* New York: International Universities Press.

Khan, R.M.M. (1974), *The Privacy of the Self.* New York: International Universities Press.

Kohut, H. (1971), *The Analysis of the Self.* New York: International Universities Press.

———— (1977), *The Restoration of the Self.* New York: International Universities Press.

Lacan, J. (1969), *Ecrits.* Editions de Seuil, Paris.

———— (1977), *Ecrits: A Selection,* W.W. Norton & Co., New York. Translated by Alan Sheridan.

Laing, R.D. (1962), *The Divided Self.* London: Penguin Books.

Peterfreund, E. (1975), The need for a new general theoretical frame of reference for psychoanalysis. *Psychoanal. Quart.,* 44:534–549.

Ricoeur, P. (1970), *Freud and Philosophy: An Essay on Interpretation.* New Haven: Yale University Press.

Schafer, R. (1976), *A New Language for Psychoanalysis.* New Haven: Yale University Press.

Stone, L. (1975), Some problems and potentialities of present-day psychoanalysis. *Psychoanal. Quart.,* 44:331–370.

Sullivan, H.S. (1953), *The Interpersonal Theory of Psychiatry,* W.W. Norton & Co., New York.

———— (1964), *The Fusion of Psychiatry and Social Science,* W.W. Norton & Co., New York.

Winnicott, D.W. (1965), *Maturational Processes and The Facilitating Environment,* New York: International Universities Press.

4

PSYCHOANALYSIS—CURE
OR PERSUASION?

EDGAR A. LEVENSON, M.D.

> When [psychoanalysis] becomes an
> institution, when it is applied to so-
> called "normal subjects," it utterly
> ceases to be a conception that can be
> justified or discussed on the basis of
> cases: it no longer cures, it persuades; it
> shapes for itself subjects who conform
> to its own interpretation of man. It
> has its converts and perhaps its rebels;
> it can no longer convince. Beyond the
> true and the false, it is a myth, and
> Freudianism thus degraded is no longer
> an interpretation, but a variant of the
> Oedipus Myth.
> Lévi-Strauss (1963, p. 196)

My most consistent interest has been the perplexing relation between what the psychoanalyst formulates about what he does and what he actually does in therapy (Levenson, 1973). And, if the process of therapy does not follow straightforwardly—as I suspect it does not—from the theory, how does the therapist know how to do what he does when he does it? Certainly it must be agreed that therapists of different persuasions all get results they deem satisfactory. Are they doing different things, or the same thing in different ways? Are there different cures? If the treatment depends on the metapsychology of the therapist, is it not just an ideological conversion? Then, what one therapist calls "cure" is nothing more than a successful proselytization: the patient is now fine according to the therapist's scriptures.

This gap between practice and theory exists in any activity that can be both performed and described. It is equally true of art, dance, or skiing. In most activities, though, the theory is understood to be no more than a temporary manual of procedure on which to lean until the process becomes automatic. Theory, in these instances, may not help, but it won't hurt either. As Frederick Crews (1976) put it, "Freud wrote [in 'On narcissism'] that 'the whole structure' of psychoanalysis stands apart from metapsychological propositions, which 'can be replaced and discarded without damaging' that structure. Freud knew that high-level theory was an afterthought to the relatively direct inferences of the consulting room" (p. 34). But in psychoanalysis the danger is that the theory becomes an ideological indoctrination *sui generis* and the patient becomes a disciple.[1] Is there a psychoanalytic cure distinct from persuasion, a unique psychoanalytic process that is something more than, or better yet, other than, the therapist's molding the patient to his particular view of man? Is the therapist's vaunted system of meanings and interpretations merely a strategy to produce the change he deems necessary? Are we involved in persuading the patient to live better without letting him know we are doing so? There has been considerable confusion throughout the history of psychoanalysis about the relation of its means to its ends; yet, how can one possibly do therapy without some system of beliefs, some structuring orientation, and, simultaneously, how can one avoid making psychoanalysis a technique of persuasion, of eliciting change in the direction selected by the therapist?

Whether the patient is seen as victim or wrong-doer doesn't much matter. Whether the therapy proceeds along the principles of Martin Buber or Machiavelli doesn't much matter. Whether the therapist is nurturing or depriving doesn't much matter. Even if the therapist exercises the greatest possible restraint, he cannot fail to see the material according to his own categories of experience and belief. It is a neo-Kantian imperative. There is no psychoanalytic neutrality, be the patient upright or horizontal, be the therapist garrulous or silent as the grave. If the therapist knows where the therapy should go and what the outcome should be, it is pari passu ideological and unavoidably persuasive. One may have a metapsychology that holds that the

---

[1] I would define ideology as a system of beliefs that explains the past, defines the present, and predicts the future. Lévi-Strauss (1963) put it very nicely when he said that a myth is a "machine for the suppression of time." Ideologies, too, take out of life all the unpredictables, contingencies, and tendencies to novelty. Newtonian clockwork predictability reigns.

patient has been mystified by family experience. The goal of therapy becomes to lift the mystification, to let the patient see that he has learned not to "know what he knows he knows." But I cannot see this as an emergent process: it is ideological conversion no matter what emphasis is put on transference. It is in the service of directed change; i.e., cure follows the patient's acceptance of the therapist's truth. Technique is the rhetoric of this process. Masud Khan (1969) has said facetiously that we obtain the patient's truth so that we can tell him the metatruth. Resistances to truth (proper meaning) are worked through, analyzed. This often becomes a series of metacommunicational ploys much as Haley (1963) has described. Moreover, it has been claimed that manipulation of the patient, or of the family milieu, is justifiable in terms of therapeutic ends. It is indeed this element of unabashed manipulation that makes some family therapy seem uncomfortably fascistic to the analytic therapist struggling to be neutral. Such therapists make the decision about what constitutes relevant living and push the patient toward it. At the other end of the continuum, one finds therapists who feel that even minimal direction is a serious political contaminant to the therapy process, that the therapist must guard against even unconsciously coloring the therapy with what he thinks matters. Various women's and homosexual groups have protested therapists' tendency to politicize improvement, to define it in terms of their own value systems.

How then can a therapist maintain neutrality? In this sense, what actually defines participant observation? Is it possible to be an observer of a process in which one is a participant? Is there something operationally paradoxical in this concept? To restate the original question, is there a therapy independent of the therapist's beliefs? Is it possible to do therapy without subtly persuading the patient to believe what you believe? What it comes to is that unless the method of arriving at the truth is at least as relevant as the truth arrived at, then, I would claim, one is pressing ideology. In other words, unless one examines the method by which one arrives at the truth and treats that as having an independent validity, separate from the truth arrived at, then one is simply indoctrinating the patient.

This may be a quite benign operation, as in the case of a patient who had quit her first therapist. The treatment was characterized by frequent serious suicidal threats. The therapist, existentially oriented, was accustomed to treasure his self-doubts as evidences of his authenticity. He was having a really difficult time dealing with this woman's suicidal threats; unsure whether he was treating her properly and whether he was competent to contain her self-destructiveness. The patient quit therapy and went on to a second analyst, a Kleinian, who was able to stand rock-solid in the face of the patient's onslaught of suicidal threats. The patient kept threatening suicide; the analyst, equally implacably, interpreted early deep dynamics. The patient recovered. Both the theoretical position of the therapist and his characterological unflappability (which may well have made the theoretical position initially sympathetic to him) combined to offer the patient the climate of conviction and faith in change that led to her improvement.

Surely some love affair exists between a theory and the characterological styles of both patient and therapist. The therapist, in writing up this case report, is very much impressed by the effectiveness of his deep direct interpretations. He feels quite sure that the truth of the interpretations triumphed. But one wonders, could it simply have been the different participation in the suicide threats? Both therapists believed they knew what mattered. Both had different conceptual frameworks. Both went about it differently. What is the explicit relation then between their theory, their practice, and the fact that an interpretation works or a patient gets better? What does that really say about the "truth" of what one tells the patient?

One must remember that an interpretation is not only a version of the truth or an understanding, but also a *participation*. There is no interpretation without participation. This dictum was, after all, Harry Stack Sullivan's great contribution to operational psychoanalysis. Every participation is a metacommunication about the content of the interpretation. Every interpretation is a message and a message about the message, as Bateson (1955) has put it. But, additionally, *the metacommunication is an enactment of the content under discussion at the time of the interpretation.* This participation is as vital a part (but no more so) of the interpretation as the spoken message.

In short, two things occur in an interpretation. The therapist formulates a truth, and in the process of telling this truth the therapist participates with the patient around this truth.

In a much quoted case of Harry Stack Sullivan's, he sees in consultation a young man who has been rapidly sinking into a schizophrenic decompensation (Sullivan, 1954, pp. 21–22). On inquiry, Sullivan notes that the patient's parents are described as being quite perfect, beyond reproach, although they have obviously stifled every move toward independence the young man has attempted. Sullivan says to himself, "Oh yeah, it doesn't sound so good to me. It doesn't make sense. Maybe you've overlooked something." Does he say that to the patient? No way! What he does say is, "I have a vague feeling that some people might doubt the utility to you of the care with which your parents, and particularly your mother, saw to it that you didn't learn to dance." Now Sullivan says, "I was delighted to see the schizophrenic young man give me a sharp look." This exchange, which I think is in language and style worthy of a Baker Street regular, has been described as technique. Havens, for instance, has written a book (1973) about Sullivanian technique and describes this particular episode as a conscious decision on Sullivan's part to approach the young man obliquely so as not to elicit excess anxiety. In other words, it is a strategy of technique that is appropriate to Sullivan's concept of the schizophrenic dilemma.

But why such a strange, crusty, Edwardian indirection so different than his first comment to himself? There are other ways of being oblique. Essentially Sullivan is making an interpretation of content. He is saying to the patient something of what he thinks the parents have done. But he is also making another interactional communication. He is saying to the patient: "I am aware that you are aware that what you are saying about your parents' beneficence is sheer baloney. You do not believe it but you expect me to believe it because you think we are all hypocrites aligned against you. I'm not stupid enough to try to be friendly toward you because you would think I'm trying to butter you up, but I thought I would let you know that I'm in on the game." Now that sounds rather more like R. D. Laing and of course it may not be what Sullivan had in mind at all. But it seems to me it is as probable as the idea that he was simply trying to spare the patient anxiety by a studied indirection. In essence it is a very complex communication to the patient about the layering-upon-layering of awareness in his life, the Laingian paradox that he doesn't know that he knows about what he doesn't know he knows.

I'm claiming that in the psychoanalytic process there is an essential force for change that does not depend alone on the truth of the professed content, the metapsychology of the therapist. Nor does it depend on the therapist's participation with the patient, but rather on a dialectical interaction of both these elements. It feels "bigger than both of us" and gives both therapist and patient a feeling of being carried along by a current of change. It doesn't help the patient to arrive at what the therapist already knows although the therapist may well know what is wrong. Nor is it exclusively a healing by encounter, although both operations take place in therapy. What human function can mediate this paradox?

Like Oedipus confronting the Sphinx, we are asked: What is inside us yet between us? What is intrinsically mine yet intrinsically yours? What is there given yet made between us? The answer, of course, is language. And my claim is that the psychoanalytic process, the healing process, is a language process which allows for, indeed requires, the synthesis of these two paradoxically oppositional aspects of therapy—the aspect of meaning and that of experience. Rather than calling it a language process, I think it might be more precise to refer to it as a semiotic process in the sense that it encompasses more than spoken language. It includes also sign systems, nonverbal cueings, distances, dispersions—the whole repertoire of interpersonal language.

Language obviates the hoary battle between inside and outside since language is, of course, both. There can be no communication without an intrapsychic language process and there can be no language without a recipient, even an imaginary recipient. Language also permits of an open resolution because the process is what can be called teleonomic, not teleological; i.e., there is no predetermined end goal although the process is goal-seeking; it is a process seeking out by continuous exchange with the environment optimum outcomes. That sounds like a mighty fine distinction, but it is the difference, as von Bertalanffy (1968) views it, between open systems theory and its explanations of biological goal-seeking (the way an open system develops, say, in an evolutionary system or a genetic system) and the final causal explanations of religion.

Thus the patient develops in therapy a solution that is not really his solution, but is also not the therapist's. Although it may or may not coincide with either one of their prior expectations, it is, in essence, a mutual solution—almost, in a Gestalt sense, a "best" configuration.

I am attempting a distinction between two kinds of interaction. One that shall describe in more detail which I label *discourse* and the other which I have described, admittedly pejoratively, as ideological indoctrination or persuasion. In an interesting book, *The Responsive Chord,* Schwartz (1973), an advertising executive, has defined the heart of persuasion (soft-selling) as what he calls "resonance." The main thrust of "resonance" is that the power of persuasion lies in reinforcing what people already believe. In other words, rather than coercing or cajoling the subject into believing something new, one picks up latent configurations and reinforces them. "The patient learns," as Lacan (1972) states, "what the therapist knows, which is what the patient already knew." In assaying persuasion, one knows what one is after, what the *desideratum* is. In discourse, there is really no script at all. One proceeds quite differently. I think it is of relevance that in the earlier works on analysis, particularly in Freud's Wolf Man (1971) when he and the patient were collaborators, explorers, not operating out of a formal structure, the therapeutic milieu seemed more spontaneous and possibly effective. Once the Procrustean theory begins to come in, the patient and the entire process is reified.

The perspective I shall describe has been the focus of structural linguists such as Barthes, Jakobson, Lévi-Strauss, and DeSaussure. It is of real significance that Freud can and has been reinterpreted in structural linguistic terms.[2] Freud discovered structuralism before structuralism discovered Freud. Both Freud and the structuralists base their programs on the analysis of surface phenomena derived from underlying structures through the interposition of transformational rules. In Freud, distortions of dream work and ego defenses constitute the principle transformations. Barthes (1970) has said, "We are all trying with different methods, styles and perhaps even prejudices to get to the core of the linguistic pact so that every moment of discourse is both absolutely new and simultaneously absolutely understood" (p. 144). It is this dialectic between understanding and newness that, I think, makes for the core of the therapeutic discourse.

Note, for the moment, that I'm talking about the structure of discourse, not the content per se. For instance, when a therapist listens to a dream, automatically he groups the data along two different lines. And the two different groupings he uses are the same groupings used in ordinary speech or that Lévi-Strauss uses to delineate cultural patterns. This is really a very difficult concept. First, the therapist deals with what is true over time, with what is consistently meaningful and remains constant. Second, he deals with what is immediately and contextually true, what is, "context-dependent," that is, the significance of any feature depends on its placement, its position in a structure. This is equally true of chess pieces, words in a sentence, or tonal or expression changes: relevance *is* contextual location. One deals with what is consistently true and one deals with what is immediately relevant.

As a very simple clinical example: a patient has three dreams together. In one dream he is dealing with his Chinese laundry man who is giving him trouble about getting his shirt back. In the second dream he is in a restaurant and, although he has a reservation, he has to wait

---

[2] See A. Wilden (1972) for a discussion of Lacan, Jakobson, Bateson, and Lévi-Strauss.

for his table. In the third dream he is in a bank, is trying to obtain a loan, and is being asked to pay some outrageous interest. The consistent theme running through all three dreams is the frustration at dealing with some functionary who is giving him a hard time. They express his difficulty with authority figures and his complex attitudes about frustration, disappointment, and disapproval. But every analyst immediately hears something else in these dreams. He hears them as transferential dreams. Why? Because inscrutability, fixed time, and money arrangements are all three strongly characteristic of the psychoanalytic setting. Now this collation occurs automatically, but the two kinds of thinking processes involved are entirely different. The first axis is the axis of the story—the manifest content. One doesn't need to know the patient to hear the message: the dreams are talking about someone who is having a lot of trouble with people who are supposed to be servicing him and are not. This first axis—the axis of what remains consistently true—is called the axis of *metaphor*. Metaphor meaning literally "to carry over." The second axis is considerably more obscure. One notes that in this case it doesn't come from the patient's associations at all. One doesn't need his association to laundry men and inscrutability. The associations could have come from him, but are not his exclusive province. They are culturally shared by both therapist and patient; the meaning is determined by social *context*. We know the meaning because we know where it fits in the context of our mutual experience. This axis is called the axis of *metonymy*.

The two axes then are metaphor and metonymy.[3] Metonymy is a variant of another rather obscure word *synecdoche* wherein a part is used to represent the whole. For instance, if one says "The Flag" one is using the flag in a synecdochic or a metonymic sense, that is, one is not just talking about that cloth object, but about patriotism, nation, and all its implications. To restate, metaphor is always independent of time and space. It is always true. Metonymy is dependent on time and space. It is true only at the moment and in context.

Since, as Barthes (1970) has said, "Discourse is no more than one great sentence," (p. 136) this dialectical process is the same that goes on in discourse with the patient. It is an innate structure, given; not a matter of choice or preference, it is consistent with the

---

[3] Edmund Leach presents an excellent exegesis of the different nomenclature used for these two axes in his little book, *Claude Lévi-Strauss* (1970). The recent (1977) English translation of Jacque Lacan's *Ecrits* also has an elaboration of the metaphor-metonomy thesis (p. 155.)

structuralist ethos of trying to examine the way ordinary knowing occurs. I am not attempting to present a way of doing psychoanalysis as a volitional inquiry. Rather, I am attempting to examine what happens when therapy is done. We use language, much as we hum tunes, quite automatically. We do not know what we are going to say until we hear ourselves say it. I suggest that the process of therapy has much this same surface unselfconsciousness, and deeper, intricate organization.

In therapy, then, one listens to the material automatically along these two lines. One listens for the metaphor that remains constant all the way through. It is there that the therapist's metapsychology is validly appropriate because one can use a variety of imagery for the metaphor. Nevertheless, as in Kafka's *Metamorphosis,* which can (and has been) given a Catholic interpretation, a Marxist interpretation, and a Freudian interpretation, the metaphor, the parable of metamorphosis, remains generally available. Metonymy, on the other hand, is the reservoir of the idiosyncratic and social experience of both the patient and the therapist. It is nonlinear; it doesn't tell a story and it doesn't increase understanding as much as it focuses temporality. It adds immediate relevance and quite often the real depth of affect.

Shifting from axis to axis is quite automatic. For instance, a dream in which a patient is struggling through mud to reach a perfect white house doesn't require much associative inquiry except to wonder why it emerges now. It's true of you as well as me; its message is evident in any patient who has the dream. It is a perfect metaphor. But if I dream of a bird with two heads and a yellow weskit, one needs associations to make any sense of it. That dream is pure metonymy; without knowing the associations that dream is utterly without any kind of meaning. It is true also that this is not either/or; it is really two ways of looking at the same phenomenon. It is the Yin/Yang of symbolism. Schizophrenics, for instance, talk almost exclusively in the metonymic axis.[4] Much the same bipolarity can be discerned in literature and poetry.

I wish to emphasize that this is not another more complicated way of describing free association. Metonymy includes the associations of *both* therapist and patient, and covers both idiosyncratic associations and commonly shared cultural associations. Moreover, free association implies an underlying truth which will be revealed by penetrating the defenses of the patient. Defenses scramble the truth; free association

---

[4] See Wilden (1972, pp. 354–364) for a discussion of schizophrenic metonomy.

reveals the metatruth that is under the truth. In the structuralist perspective, the truth is never arrived at; rather, it keeps changing as the
process proceeds. One does not arrive at a static reductive truth, one
simply deals with an emergent increasingly complex reality.

Let me use another dream as an example of this. A patient dreams
of eating his hat. I'll omit most of the details, but the point of the
dream is that he describes the hat as made of "polymer urethane."
In the dream he thinks, "Funny, it doesn't taste like rubber." I've
chosen this dream because it·illustrates the different parameters of
metaphor and metonymy and their overlap. There are many associative
links: for example, the patient works for a chemical firm. There are
even associations to chewing on his hat. But one need not know anything about this man to know that the metaphor for eating one's hat
is some kind of an act of contrition or losing a bet and paying off. Yet
there are other metaphoric issues. Anybody old enough to remember
the Thirties remembers it was a very common visual theme in the
comic strips and movies. This man is visually oriented, he is old enough
and quite witty. So one might think either the reference is somewhat
anachronistic, it is not a term people use much anymore, or perhaps
it sets the time period of the relevant historical experience. But still
more, examine the logic of the dream. He eats the hat, he tastes the
hat and says to himself, "Funny, it doesn't taste like rubber." This is
precisely the logic of the Mad Hatter's tea party when the Mad Hatter
is trying to repair his watch with butter and Alice says to him, "You
can't fix a watch with butter" and he dips it in the tea and comments
wistfully, "But it was the very best butter."

Now those are not free associations nor are they even associations
particularly relevant to the patient's private experience. But they are
the kind of play I think most therapists do. Once one catches the zany
Alice-in-Wonderland logic of the dream, the therapist suddenly realizes
that he and the patient have been having exactly this kind of exchange;
that it goes on all the time when one speaks with this man. He goes
off in this funny kind of oblique, paralogical negativism. The metaphor
of the dream then has meaning not just for the dream, but for the
carrying over of its patterning into the transference, into the other
areas of the patient's life. In other words, they are transforms of each
other. The metaphor "carries over," which is what metaphors are
meant to do. Moreover, once one has heard the metaphor and extended
it with the metonymic associations, the patient never seems the same
again and one never hears what he is saying exactly the way one has

heard it before. And what's more, one has absolutely no choice in the matter. Something has occurred in the therapy.

To recapitulate, metaphor is ideological but necessary; one must have some way of talking about things. Metonymy is totally contextual, either immediately personal or cultural, but it is equally necessary.[5]

If the therapist says, "I think you are afraid of having positive feelings toward your mother," the metaphor is clear enough. At least the coding of the message is clear. This occasion has a similarity to many others in your life. It is manifested by the same sequence of tentative offering of love, double-bind response, dissociation, and then anger displaced to some other area. Transformationally, the same sequence occurs in the session, in your dream in which you were telling me about your husband, and now with me. But there is an additional message which can be only abstracted from the total semiotic context. Even a stenographic transcript won't give it to you. Let's suppose the therapist says all this in a kindly fashion, without accusation, with the firm conviction that he is not feeling rebuffed. This is a quite different communication than if he had arrived at the insight by first feeling distracted, bored, recognizing his own anger, and then backtracking to realize that the patient had rejected his efforts to be responsive. It is the same metaphoric configuration of events, but it is entered from a different direction and played out from a different starting point.

Let's suppose as a third possibility that the therapist is really offended, doesn't contact his own anger, but makes the same interpretation as a doctrinary gesture. The observer might see a different metacommunicational set. The therapist would be smiling kindly, but there would be a slightly icy tone to his voice: the patient would look vaguely uneasy. So, the full message requires not simply the knowledge of content, of the metaphor, of what the therapist is saying to the patient, but also the immediate contextual framework. The metaphor remains consant and moreover it is correct, even if the therapist says it out of pique,

---

[5] There is some reason to believe there may be a neurological substratum for this description. Pribram, Lurie, and Jakobson have described two areas of the left brain, in the language cortex, each area of which roughly approximates one of these two different functions. And Luria has described a series of aphasias in which one of these functions is lost and not the other; for example, where the person knows the function of a coin but can't name it. Or can name it but doesn't know the function of it: the function of an object being essentially metonymic (Pribram, 1971).

out of countertransference. The effect of the interpretation will differ, though, depending on *who* the therapist is in the transferential situation as he makes the interpretation. Bateson's "metacommunication" is, in the patient-therapist relationship, the metonymic clue to the posture of the therapist (therapist as good mother, bad mother, good father, sibling, etc.). Without this situation-dependent clue, the onlooker cannot know what the whole message is.

Interpretations of content without context degenerate into cliché or indoctrination. If one listens to a patient and simply interprets what one conceives to be the truth, an indoctrination results. Interpretations of context without content occur frequently in therapies concerned with authentic exchanges. I think that can be equally disastrous since, without being anchored into any system of explanations, one gets essentially spontaneous acting out between the therapist and the patient, never anchored in any structure of comprehension. If one believes in insight or truth, one believes that the patient must hear the truth of what is being said to him about himself and that this truth must bypass or work through his defenses. Insight in the sense of sight into his own head is required. If one believes that immediacy is all, then one believes that it is the experience with the therapist that is healing. The words don't really matter as much as the quality and authenticity of the exchange. I think both these views are correct, but I think they are both actually incomplete. They are the Siamese twins of psychotherapy: inseparable and irreconcilable.

Why do patients change in therapy as viewed from this perspective? I'll put it in the most condensed form first and then elaborate.[6] The transfer of data from the metonymic to the metaphoric axis permits an open system to move and change. In other words, when what is contextual and immediate becomes transferred into permanent metaphor and integrated into the recurrent patterning of the patient, change has occurred. Now this has equivalence with what Piaget says in his concept of assimilation and accommodation. Assimilation and accommodation are really the same two axes of change. Changing the metaphor is changing the basic wiring of a person's self-system. I don't mean changing the imagery of the metaphor but its basic organization. One could use libido-theory language or interpersonal language without changing the basic metaphor one bit. It would be really a matter of old wine in new bottles. For change to occur, material that emerges

---

[6] See Wilden (1972, chapter XII) for a detailed presentation of open-systems change.

from the metonymic dimension must enlarge and change the metaphor. The metaphor is heard differently, as in the instance of the dream with the hat. The therapist, hearing the meaning differently, changes his participation automatically. He *sees* the patient differently. His changed participation changes the metonymic axis which changes the metaphor which changes the metonymic axis and so change hitches along, like an inchworm.

Let me give you an example of this: the patient is a man in his thirties. He is talking about his mother critically and complains that she is an obsessive, humorless, self-righteous woman. She has irritated the entire family by her dim-witted devotion to large liberal causes. He sounds derisive and amused by her. This, one notes, was the tone of the family exchanges when she held forth and he and his sister and father listened with amusement and contempt. Transferentially he is now talking to the therapist-as-father. The therapist is listening lightly, amused by his presentation. He is not blank, serious, appalled, or even questioning the patient's derisiveness. The patient is saying how his mother collected reams of newspaper and magazine articles to bolster her continuous contentiousness. He says, "She collected in paper bags. For God's sake, *brown* paper bags," and he begins to laugh and laugh and laugh. The laughter gets out of control and begins to sound desperate. The therapist hears that "brown paper bags" is the tip of an iceberg of metonymic meaning. The therapist sits solemnly now listening to the patient's increasing laughter. Suddenly, the patient begins to cry helplessly. Why? "I don't know. It just makes me feel terrible. Brown paper bags for Christ sake." The therapist says something like, "It sounds like you feel sorry for your mother." Which, by the way, may not be true, but it is essentially a sympathetic response to the man's crying. Now one could say, so what? The patient's feelings broke through his defenses of detached amusement. True, but it took a metonymic "brown paper bags" to do it. Not paper bags mind you, but *brown* paper bags—a condensation of "bag-lady," those derelict ladies in New York who haunt the garbage cans carrying their belongings, and brown bagging, a phrase used for carrying one's lunch to school because one couldn't afford to buy it. If his mother had collected her data in a Bendel tote I don't think the tearfulness would have been precipitated. Note that the metaphor was: "I'm having a hard time getting away from my sticky, opinionated, castrating mother." The metonymic clue was brown paper bags. Note that the transference was at first: "You are Daddy and we collude in making fun of Mommy. We know what a pain she is." The therapist goes along. The metonymic clue, the subsequent change in affect, changes the therapist's participation. He now hears the message differently. He hears: "I am vulnerable to my feelings. I feel profoundly ashamed of and very sorry for my poor mother who is the butt of our humor." If the therapist had laughed, the material would have stopped, but hearing it differently changes his participation. He now does not collude against the mother, but says to the patient, in essence, "It's all right, Daddy is saying so, for you to feel sorry. It doesn't make you a sissy. See, I can show compassion and caring too." Thus the therapist's perception of the patient and his perception of himself interacting with the patient have changed. In other words, a shift has occurred that doesn't have to be spelled out by either one of them. It has happened to both of them and I think one would be hard put to know exactly why "brown paper bags" precipitated the incident except that it is in some way a very specific, highly charged, metonymic clue. It doesn't have to do entirely with the mechanisms of repression because one sees the same release of feeling and memory in Proust or in Schachtel's work on childhood memory. What seemed to be very, very casual cues set off an entire associative complex. This is more than just eliciting a dissociated affect or working through an anxiety-laden incident. The change persists because we have effected a change in our own metaphor and, if we fail to do this, we stay where we are. In a certain sense this isn't far from Harry Stack Sullivan's concept that the self-system is made up of reflected appraisals. The therapist is not in any sense a passive mirror for the reflected appraisals. It is much more of an active exchange between the two.

Many other possible interpretations exist for that exchange with the therapist. There are many ways of getting at whatever the repressed affect was. Concern, shame, disgust, disappointment in his mother could have been elicited in a variety of other ways. Therapists will automatically re-edit, correct, translate this vignette, perhaps seeing the right way to do it. But as far as I can see the therapist is never in the position of clearly knowing once and for all what anything means. This process of discourse, as I have described it, has one tremendous saving grace: as long as the process is proceeding, the content is relatively unimportant. That is, starting with a variety of interpretations and metonymic cues, we all arrive at some further point along the developmental trajectories available to the patient. This is what von Bertalanffy (1968) in *General Systems Theory* called the principle of *equifinality*: open systems, no matter where one starts, if permitted to develop and move, will move along the trajectories available to them in terms of their own general programing. Therapists starting from different positions and with different interactions can elicit similar changes in the patient.

It is worth noting that affect is at the call of the metonyomic, not of the metaphoric. One usually trips the affect in the process of eliciting these iceberg-tip cueing exchanges. I think that is one of the limitations of metaphoric interpretation. It is very useful, inasmuch as it teaches the patient about the way he lives, but it doesn't have much emotional impact. It seems very likely that metonomy calls on a deeper, more "analogic" process, with obscure but very pervasive connections. Metaphor is a more "digital" process, more linear and intellectual. There are some interesting implications, playfully at least, for the left brain (digital)/right brain (analogic) theorists (Ornstein, 1972).

To review the argument: If we assume that psychoanalytic change depends on the specific truth and the relevance of the therapists formulations or beliefs, then I think we are on the razor's edge of ideology. Therapeutic technique becomes a technique for helping the patient arrive at insight, which will be acceptance of the therapist's truth. What is this if not the art of persuasion? It may not be the truth arrived at, as much as the manner of arriving at the truth that is the essence of therapy. This process of arriving at the truth has a structure that is linguistic in nature. With a therapist willing to listen in the most profound sense of the word, certain lines of inquiry will be followed. The therapist will identify patterns and configurations of events. He will pattern events, over time and across the present, including his own interactions with the patient, the transference, dreams, the history, and any other material the therapy encompasses. These patterns are endlessly repeated over and over again in larger and smaller events.[7] This constancy, this search for transformational sameness or metaphor is perhaps the most striking feature of human efforts to make sense of the world, from paleolithic scratchings on tusks all the way up to the computer technology of the present. Heisenberg (1970) said "Patterns in our mind may reflect the internal structure of the world. The language of images, metaphors and similes is probably the only way to approach the one from wider regions" (quoted by Laing, 1976). Simply put, the oldest of human endeavors is the search for constancy,

---

[7] See my holographic model (Levenson, 1976). One can find the same patterns folded into any ten minutes of the therapy session. Many good therapists can take ten minutes of a session or a dream and explicate an entire experience with the patient from it.

for recurring patterns, for metaphor. But one also learns not to count on constancy if one wishes to survive. So one looks for shift, for changes, for novelty.

Metaphor, like myth, is a mnemonic device. It is a way for dealing with constancy. Metonymy is a device for dealing with change. So, the two faces of reality are constancy and change; being and becoming; truth and relevance; code and context; metaphor and metonymy.

I have tried to suggest that analysis is in the mainstream of structuralist theory and its more popular offspring in this country, general systems theory. It is a dialectical linguistic process and subject to the rules of that process. Human language and perhaps human survival is dependent on an integration of the search for timeless pattern and the detection of imminent change. It is this out-of-balanceness that makes for movement and keeps us neither as ephemeral as the May fly nor as perfectly immutable as the shark. The same deceptively simple process motivates vast systems of biological and ecological change from genetics to evolution. Any analyst of any persuasion must follow this same dialogic process to be effective. Every institute has both its idealogues and its hunch players, but, in the end, therapy really is integration of both. There is a Sufi saying: "Don't learn, listen." It's not bad advice, but it's not easy either.

REFERENCES

Barthes, R. (1970), To Write: An Intransitive Verb. In: R. Macksey and E. Donato, *The Structuralist Controversy*. Baltimore: Johns Hopkins Press.

Bateson, G. (1955), The message "This is play." *Transactions of the Second Conference on Group Processes*. New York: J. Macy Foundation, pp. 145–242.

Crews, F. (1976), *The New York Review of Books*. Feb. 5, p. 34.

Havens, L. (1973), *Approaches to the Mind*. Boston: Little, Brown.

Haley, J. (1963), *Strategies of Psychotherapy*. New York: Grune & Stratton.

Heisenberg, W. (1970), *Natural Law and the Structure of Matter*. London: The Rebel Press, pp. 44–45.

Khan, M. (1969), Introduction to Marion Milner, *The Hands of the Living God*. New York: International Universities Press.

Lacan, J. (1972), quoted by Wilden, A. in *Systems & Structure: Essays in Communication & Exchange*. London: Tavistock.

Lacan, J. (1977), *Ecrits: a selection*. New York: W.W. Norton.

Laing, R.D. (1976), *The Facts of Life*. New York: Pantheon.

Leach, E. (1970), *Claude Lévi-Strauss*. New York: Viking Press.

Levenson, E. (1972), *The Fallacy of Understanding*. New York: Basic Books.

—— (1976), A holographic model of psychoanalytic change. *Contemp. Psychoanal.*, 12:1–20.

Lévi-Strauss, C. (1963), *Structural Anthropology*. New York: Basic Books.

Ornstein, R. (1972), *The Psychology of Consciousness*. New York: Viking Press.

Pribram, K. (1971), *Language of the Brain*. Englewood Cliffs, N.J.: Prentice-Hall.

Sullivan, H.S. (1954), *The Psychiatric Interview,* ed. H.S. Perry & M.I. Gawel. New York: W.W. Norton.

Schwartz, T. (1973), *The Responsive Chord*. New York: Anchors Press.

von Bertalanffy, L. (1968), *General Systems Theory*. New York: Braziller.

Wilden, A. (1972), *System and Structure—Essays in Communication and Exchange*. London: Tavistock.

Wolfman (1971), *The Wolfman,* ed. by Gardiner, M. New York: Basic Books.

5

SLEEP AND DREAMS IN PRACTICE

E. S. TAUBER, M.D.

IN THIS chapter I shall present an overview of my own studies on sleep and dreams followed by a brief statement of the contributions of several investigators whose work has far-reaching significance for psycho-therapists. I shall conclude with a section on the fugue state—which has provoked much speculation on my part. My hypothesis is that fugue states can exist in forms so subtle that they may escape attention. These fugue states reflect the psychophysiological characteristics of certain sleep disorders which, paradoxically, are also disorders of wake-fulness. At the present time our methodology and technical instrumenta-tion are not sufficiently developed to verify or refute this hypothesis, yet, I believe it has some merit.

By way of introduction to my own research studies, I want to make two points of practical interest. First, somewhat over 20 years ago, with the discovery by Aserinsky and Kleitman (1953) of what we call rapid-eye-movement (REM) sleep, it became clear to imaginative investigators that an extraordinary finding had come to light. It was not that no one had observed this phenomenon of eye mobility before; rather, these curious eye movements were previously considered evi-dence of wakefulness and as such not regarded as anything novel. By careful attention to other concomitant physiological parameters, in-cluding the elevated arousal threshold during these episodes, Aserinsky and Kleitman realized that the observed organismic state was that of sleep and not wakefulness. This exciting discovery quickly generated much research and mushrooming of literature here and abroad.

Second, with the burgeoning forth of articles, reviews, and abstracts, the Brain Information Service (BIS) took on the formidable challenge of making up-to-date information available to sleep researchers. Sleep Bulletins and Sleep Reviews now include citations from the literature of all countries where published material is available. In addition, BIS provides an excellent computerized retrieval service. BIS has organized topics into subcategories covering neurophysiology, biochemistry, pharmacology, ontogeny, phylogeny, behavior, dreaming, dream recall, patterns of dream content, biological rhythms, personality and psychopathology, and so on. An excellently indexed volume entitled *Sleep Research* is published yearly by the Brain Information Service, Brain Research Institute, UCLA, Los Angeles, California.

As I intend to show, my primary interest in psychoanalytic theory in terms of research has been along lines of exploring the psychophysiological processes involved in the analytic transaction—that is, what goes on in the doctor-patient relationship. My inquiry has been structured to illuminate processes best described as inadvertent, unconscious or preconscious, unwitting and novel. I have not myself been directly concerned, for example, with confirming or disconfirming the validity of major theoretical constructs. I do not wish to imply that what has not been congenial to my specific scientific curiosity is less worthy of study, but merely to establish my own center of engagement.

My earliest concern with process expressed itself via the avenue of dreams. This led eventually to its role in the doctor-patient relationship and specifically into the nature of countertransference phenomena (Tauber, 1952, 1954; Tauber and Green, 1959). I shall not review or summarize my contributions in that area, but prefer to move on to a later interest, namely, color in dreams, as part of what I call the discovery of "givens." In other words, while psychodynamic aspects of color in dreams are valuable for analysis, what about the incidence of color percepts in dreams and how is color integrated in other neural mechanisms aside from psychopathology?

We have to acquire basic information concerning perceptual physiology during sleep to assist us in sorting out normative data from psychopathologic data and dynamic factors. We know now that forgetting dreams is not necessarily resistance. Dreaming occurs in everyone (particularly sharply in REM sleep, but also during N-REM sleep with different phenomenal characteristics). The nature of memory and decay of memory, however, add important dimensions for study, which force us to modify our earlier simplistic, often judgmental attitudes.

In our review of the literature on color in dreams, Dr. Maurice Green and I (1962) noted that Freud had said little on the subject, and the questionnaire technique employed by Calvin Hall (1951) seemed misleading for methodological reasons. We therefore concentrated on a more subtle clinical approach to the subject. We noted that color in dreams was quite common, but that it was underreported. Since dreams contain the perceptual data of wakefulness, and since we live in a world of color, it seemed strange that color was so infrequently spontaneously reported. We suspected that it was underreported because of its lack of salience in waking life. We are all sensitive to configurational cues that are highly adaptive, and color cues are relatively inadequate as adaptive cues. It is well known that when asked to describe a stranger, one rarely recalls the color of his tie. Research into responses to stabilized images reveals that the stimulus array quickly fades; the interesting finding, however, is that the color in the viewed pattern fades out before the configurational characteristics of the design. This finding supports the common failure to acquire or retain recall of color cues. Nevertheless, we have observed that where color is of adaptive significance to the person in his daily life, it is less frequently underreported in dream recall, and if unattended to, is quickly "learned" when the subject matter is casually discussed in analysis. I will not digress at this point to discuss the complex problem of patient compliance; however, I believe that our study strongly suggests that physiological factors outweigh psychological and emotional factors.

One area of sleep research that has intrigued me is the ontogenetic and phylogenetic aspects of dreaming sleep. The early studies of many researchers were dedicated to determining clearly the physiological and psychological characteristics of dreaming sleep, referred to as REM sleep (paradoxical, rhombencephalic sleep, or active sleep). These characteristics differed markedly from those of N-REM sleep in man both physiologically and psychologically. (Of course, in animals only the physiological parameters can be studied.) Many researchers have in fact suggested that we live out three organismic states—wakefulness, N-REM sleep, and REM sleep. This tripartite division of states is a useful construct even though it is not inviolate, that is, there are overlaps.

Researchers have wondered whether dreaming sleep is characteristic of all vertebrates. At first it was thought that dreaming sleep would be present throughout the animal kingdom since the important neural processes subserving REM sleep were found to be in the brain stem. Mammalian studies quickly revealed that both REM and N-REM are present in placentals and marsupials, with one exception: REM sleep is not reported for the spiny anteater, a monotreme, although there is clear-cut evidence of N-REM sleep. I do not believe that a definitive answer with respect to REM sleep in the monotreme will be forthcoming until further specialized studies are conducted. Investigators now agree that REM sleep is present in birds (Rojas-Ramirez and Tauber, 1970). Controversy concerning the presence of REM sleep in reptiles exists (Tauber, Roffwarg, and Weitzman, 1966; Tauber, Rojos-Ramirez, and Hernandez-Peon, 1968). Again, however, one encounters new problems in studying animals in the vertebrate classes below mammals—in part because their neural organization differs significantly in certain respects from that of mammals, and because the criteria used to specify REM sleep are primarily for mammals. Although there appears to be a rest-activity cycle in amphibians, there is no clear-cut evidence of REM sleep. In my study with Dr. Weitzman of certain Bermuda reef fish, we reported evidence of eye movements during behavioral inactivity. We made detailed behavioral and physiological observations of two families of diurnal foveate fish—wrasses and parrot fish—and noted during the dark phase of the light-dark cycle independent (nonconjugate) eye movements during periods of prolonged inactivity (Tauber, 1972, 1974; Tauber and Weitzman, 1969). Correlated in time was evidence of irregular respiratory rate and decreased responsiveness to alerting stimuli, manifested by a tolerance of handling. Fish compose the largest class in the vertebrate kingdom, including over 40,000 species, while the class of mammals comprises roughly 2,400 species; thus the fish radiation is very broad with evidence of great specialization. The fact that some species of fish never sleep is well known; whether microsleep occurs, thereby protecting these fish from exhaustion, is unknown. Until recently it was incorrectly assumed that fish without swim bladders must continuously swim to avoid drowning. So far no experimental techniques have been devised to shed light on these questions, and chronic all-night electrographic studies conventionally employed in sleep research have not been successfully employed in studies of marine or fresh water species (Tauber, 1974).

More recently my colleagues and I have carried out a study to determine whether vestibular stimulation could elicit nystagmus during different sleep stages, but particularly during REM sleep, similar to that classically found during alert wakefulness. (Tauber et al., 1972). It is well known that behavioral responsiveness to sensory modalities is depressed during sleep. We observed that at no time during REM sleep was nystagmus evoked by vestibular stimulation. In addition, no clear nystagmic responses were elicited during N-REM stages 2, 3, and 4. In all stages of sleep, rotation of the torsion swing always produced slow, compensatory, conjugative eye movements. With the onset of rotational stimulation during the REM sleep stage, REM bursts were suppressed but emerged immediately following termination of stimulation; however, phasic activity of the chin muscles was unaffected by rotational stimulation during REM sleep. This experiment revealed that (1) as with other sensory modalities, vestibular response is suppressed during sleep; and (2) the phasic activity associated with vestibular stimulation is dissociated during REM sleep, i.e., although there is suppression of rapid eye movements, characteristic bursts of jaw muscle contractions are not altered in this state. Since eye-movement bursts and dreaming are temporally correlated, as a future research project it would be interesting to determine whether vestibular stimulation during REM sleep suppresses or alters dreaming.

It has been pointed out that in normal, healthy young adults sleep suppresses nystagmus induced by vestibular stimulation. During another sleep study we observed that nystagmus resulting from a central nervous system lesion disappears once sleep supervenes (Tauber et al., 1973). The literature further reveals that congenital nystagmus, a neurological disorder where nystagmus is present throughout wakefulness, also disappears during sleep. All these findings indicate that experimentally induced nystagmus and endogenous nystagmus are under the control of the sleep mechanisms.

The previous illustration dealt with experimental manipulation of sleep mechanisms on sensory input. I would now like briefly to mention a study concerned with the influence of sleep on motor mechanisms. It is well known that tremors, choreic, and athetotic movements, and, in fact, most involuntary movements tend to disappear when sleep supervenes. However, spasticity, a concomitant of hemiplegia associated with lesions of the supranuclear pathways and consistently present during wakefulness, has not been carefully studied during sleep until recently. My collaborators and I found that all skeletal and trunk muscles manifest an absence of tonic electromyographic activity throughout all stages of nocturnal sleep (Tauber, Coleman, and Weitzman, 1977). On the contrary, it appears that peripheral lesions producing, for example, fasciculations or hemi-facial spasm, survive during sleep. This suggests that the influence of sleep on motor mechanisms is selective, and that lesions of the anterior horn cells and peripheral motor nerves escape the influence of sleep. We still do not know enough about the neurophysiology of sleep to account for these findings.

A number of years ago, Ivo Kohler and others studying the effects of altered perceptual worlds accomplished their tasks by the use of prisms and an assortment of lenses which distorted the visual input. Their subjects wore these distorting spectacles for long periods of time. Briefly, they found varying degrees of adaptation were possible, first behavioral adaptation and later perceptual adaptation. Removal of the lenses produced interesting counterdisplacements for a short time, after which visual perception returned to normal. This led my colleagues and me to wonder whether altering color input would influence the dream's perceptual world. Since REM sleep seemed to share certain psychophysiological characteristics with wakefulness, we asked, for example, if a subject wore red goggles for a number of days, how that might affect his dreams. Would his dream world be influenced at all? Would, perhaps, the dream world become red or would it emerge in complementary color, namely blue-green? This is a long, complex story involving several colleagues and is reported in detail elsewhere (Roffwarg et al., 1976).

The subject wore red goggles during wakefulness. These goggles permitted transmissions of a limited range of wavelengths roughly 600–640 mμ. The blue-green part of the spectrum was blocked. The effect on the color experience in the dreams of the first night was immediate. The dreams of the first REM period replicated the goggle world, but subsequent REM dreams of the first night did not show the effect. However, each subsequent night revealed a progressive invasion of the goggle world so that after the fourth and fifth night all REM periods showed unequivocal evidence of the goggle effect, namely, reddish-orange coloration. The finding was striking: the proportion of goggle-screened colors declined sharply as the proportion of admitted wavelengths increased its loading. Final data from control studies and certain modifications in procedure are called for before complete assurance is attained, permitting us to attribute the results to an alteration in the subjects' perceptual environment rather than in subject expectation or suggestion. One other remarkable finding was that on the first recovery night—i.e., after removal of goggles—the goggle effect completely vanished. This latter response could not be unambiguously predicted and will require further investigation. Consideration must be given to issues well known in psychology, such as the recency phenomenon, as well as the role of short- and long-term memory and memory decay in respect to the processing of dreams.

The various forms of memory and memory decay are important for the theory and practice of psychoanalysis. Since memory is so central to optimum human functioning and essential for the laboratory of the therapeutic transaction, it is imperative that memory receive high priority in sleep research. From the beginning, dreams—dream recall and forgetfulness—have comprised the modeling clay from which psychoanalysis sculpts its story of man's nature. The more recent study of its neurophysiological substrate has further contributed to our understanding of man's nature. Simply put, psychoanalysis and neurophysiology have converged on the dream state—the REM state. This scientific collaboration has enriched the dimension of the inquiry and has generated new hypotheses and fresh questions. A most provocative hypothesis has been the suggestion that maturation is facilitated and enhanced by the endogenous stimulation occurring in dreaming sleep (Roffwarg, Muzio, and Dement, 1966). But we are now ready to search for hypotheses that lend themselves better to empirical testing, a basic aim of science. The study of memory fulfills the requirements of such a model.

One recent study deals with paradoxical sleep and memory storage processes (Fishbein and Gutwein, 1977). Their abstract reads as follows:

> This paper advances the view that during the paradoxical sleep (PS) phase, the brain sets in motion a chain-of-events that is necessary for learning ability and that these events are an integral component of memory storage processes. The evidence supporting the position taken in this paper comes from experiments showing that: (1) PS deprivation (PSD), prior to training, or immediately thereafter, impairs the formation of a permanent memory trace; (2) prolonged PSD following learning interferes with the state of a consolidated memory trace; (3) in the course of distributed learning, each learning session is followed by a brief augmentation of PS; (4) massed learning, in which registration of a learned response is incomplete, is followed by a protracted augmentation of PS; (5) pharmacological alterations of brain protein systhesis, cholinergic and catecholaminergic neurotransmitter activity are paralleled by the appearance or disappearance of PS periods, with concomitant changes in memory trace. The accumulated data suggest that the events occurring during the PS phase play an integral part in memory storage processes in two ways:
>
> (1) Provide conditions which facilitate the conversion of a learned response into a stable, long-term memory, and (2) actively maintain the stability of a consolidated memory trace.

In order to gain a broad perspective over sleep and wakefulness, one readily notes that this alternation of state is controlled by a biological clock, the period of which is approximately 24 hours. This biological cycle or rhythm is called circadian because it is not exactly a 24-hour cycle. Many cycles exist in nature, and there are cycles within cycles. Those cycles less than 24 hours are called ultradian (e.g., the sleep-dream cycle), and cycles longer than a day (e.g., menstrual cycle) are called infradian. Neurophysiological and biochemical processes have a rhythmic character and can be entrained by geophysical events such as light and darkness. J. Allan Hobson (1975) has contributed an excellent formulation of biological rhythms with specific focus on the sleep-dream cycle. His article clearly exposes the nature of the interaction of these rhythms and is essential reading for a truly informed overview.

Sleep disorders laboratories and clinics have come into existence because modern sleep research has progressed to the point where one can expect now to study problems of clinical urgency such as insomnia and other sleep disorders. Whether these conditions are more frequent than they were is perhaps irrelevant, but because of the advances in knowledge and technology it is possible to define, diagnose, and treat these conditions more successfully.

The role of drugs in the treatment of insomnia has received extensive study, and the Kales (1974) and their associates, among others, have observed that many hypnotics lose their effectiveness within a few weeks of continued use. In addition, they have called attention to side-effects and withdrawal responses. They have shown that the management of insomnia is difficult and each case must be studied in its own right. Sleep disorders such as somnambulism, enuresis, hypersomnia, nocturnal myoclonus, sleep apnea, both central and obstructive, and night terrors and nightmare need careful clinical and laboratory analysis for us to come to grips with these widespread disorders.

In conclusion, I want to discuss the fugue state since I have come to suspect that this condition may exist in a form that does not reflect the dramatic characteristics enumerated in literature. I shall introduce the subject by reviewing two papers dealing with the subject from different points of view.

In a psychophysiological study of fugues reported by Rice and Fisher (1976), the authors make "an attempt to establish a psychophysiological link between fugue states and sleep-dream mechanisms." Fugue states have been variously classified; however, they all manifest altered states of consciousness. Altered states of consciousness can be caused by certain types of brain lesions, drugs, alcohol, and sleep and emotional trauma which may facilitate the surfacing of a dissociated state.

Rice and Fisher present the case of a 46-year-old, married, devout Jewish male who became severely agitated and depressed several months after the death of his father. The patient, in his twenties, suffered his first fainting attack during his wife's first pregnancy. He regained consciousness within a half-hour, but appeared to be dazed for the next three days. He had complete amnesia for the entire episode. Syncopal attacks continued over the years followed by amnestic periods lasting seconds to weeks. Neurological studies revealed no abnormality, and these spells were diagnosed as idiopathic epilepsy or hysterical reaction.

The patient functioned well despite these fainting spells and episodes of amnesia until the illness of his parents, who both suffered cerebral vascular accidents within a few months of each other. Thereafter the patient was totally concerned with the care of his parents. Shortly after the death of his mother, the patient had a grand mal seizure while being examined by his internist because of chest pain. His father died soon thereafter, and 13 months later the patient was hospitalized for his depression and received electroconvulsive therapy and psychotherapy. Follow-up studies revealed that his fainting spells were really fugal states occurring late at night, at which time he would get out of bed, dress, leave his home, and disappear for hours before returning. There was amnesia for these events, and when he was informed about these activities, he was shocked and frightened and tried to deny them.

A series of all-night sleep recordings in the sleep laboratory was carried out although previous encephalogram recordings were normal. The authors report that there were two short episodes of sleep talking during predormescence, and alpha activity was recorded. Sleep talking also occurred when the patient was awakened out of REM sleep by a buzzer. The transcript of the tape recordings revealed intense verbal preoccupation with his father and his father's illness and death. In their discussion the authors infer that the sleep-talking episodes were the nocturnal equivalents of the daytime fugues, resembling them in mental content, but differing in the absence of motility. It must be remembered that this experiment was conducted in a sleep laboratory, and investigators have consensually observed that motor behavior characteristic of nocturnal episodes in the home is not replicated in the laboratory. It is highly probable that the dissociated episodes were similarly provoked, but one cannot be completely certain.

I believe we have to note that EEG evidence indicated that the patient was not electrographically asleep once the episodes became overt. Nevertheless, the immediate precursor was a state of elevated arousal threshold. It is generally conceded that sleep talking occurs during an alpha EEG, yet is associated with REM sleep or a particular N-REM stage of sleep. Thus it seems that the fugal episodes issued out of a state of drowsiness during wakefulness, predormescence, or REM sleep. *It would have been interesting to have tested the patient with the buzzer during N-REM sleep,* thereby differentiating the influence of these two sleep states where mentation is so strikingly different (see below). The authors suggest a cognitive carry-over from the REM state to the post-REM state. There seemed to be a vivid, dreamlike hallucinatory quality to the patterning of the response, similar to the quality of REM dream material. One other point made was the incorporation of the stimulus, the buzzer, during REM sleep, a common occurrence in REM sleep but also reported for N-REM sleep.

Approaching the subject of fugue and sleep disorders from a different viewpoint, Roger J. Broughton (1968), in an extremely valuable paper on certain types of sleep disorders—namely, nocturnal enuresis, somnambulism, sleep terrors, and nightmares—suggests most persuasively by ingenious experimental designs that (1) we are dealing with disorders of arousal and (2) that these disorders are not associated with dreaming sleep. This paper clearly defines what advances have been made in recent research into these disorders and sharpens our understanding of why we are still unable to treat these conditions.

First of all, Broughton shows us that "physiological differences from normal subjects, or a type predisposing the individual to a particular attack pattern, are present *throughout* the night." Furthermore, one or more of these disorders is not infrequently seen in the same individual. This finding hints at the possibility of a common disorder. The study of visual evoked potentials, the employment of indwelling catheterization for recording bladder-contraction patterns, and cardio-respiratory techniques reveal that there are distinct abnormal response patterns in these subjects as against matched controls. Employing these same experimental techniques during REM sleep rules out any connection with that sleep stage. Of course, these studies do not preclude the possibility that mentation, i.e., mental activity of great significance, may be implicated.

As is well known, dream recall is much lower for awakenings out of N-REM sleep than for those out of REM sleep. Broughton and others claim five to ten percent dream recall from N-REM sleep; other investigators, however, claim between 50 and 70 per cent dream recall from N-REM (see below). Whether the per cent of dream recall for subjects with sleep disorders is the same as for normals has, to Broughton's knowledge, not been reported. Since arousal in these cases erases most of the recollection of these attacks, one would expect dream recall to suffer equally seriously. Broughton suggests that these disorders may arise from a "psychological void," and that even symptoms specific to the attack types are due to abnormally marked physiological responses during the recurrent slow-wave arousal episode: bladder contraction producing enuresis; sensorium impairment, leading to somnambulism; and cardiorespiratory changes, giving rise to terror. Thus, Broughton concludes that with the data available, including the physiologic studies reported in his article, sleep disorders are disorders of arousal.

However, this is not the last word on the sleep disorders. Studies in Fisher's laboratory (1976) reveal that the incidence of spontaneous dream recall during N-REM sleep achieves a mean of 58 per cent, while Arkin (1970) in his investigations into nonspontaneous dream recall from stage 3–4 awakenings reports 61.5 per cent recall and Foulkes (1962) reports 70 per cent. As mentioned above, Broughton's figures run between five and ten per cent. Furthermore, Fisher has reported that percentage dream recall for his clinical group was essentially the same as that found in normal subjects.

One can see immediately that the disparity in findings with respect to dream recall percentages in Broughton's laboratory and the data from other laboratories raises certain questions. It is agreed by all that mental content in N-REM sleep may usher in the arousal, characterized by autonomic activation, sleep talking, cries, screams, etc., and the return of motility. The amnesia that accompanies these episodes makes it impossible to determine the concordance between mental content and postarousal phenomena. Fisher asserts that in certain instances he has found sequences that are not scenes activated during arousal, but are allied to prior dream content. It is recognized that content may be elaborated during the postarousal period. Fisher writes: "It is our impression that the terrifying content of the night terror often revolves around pregenital and Oedipal content relating to primal scene experiences or fantasies with projection of intense murderous, oral sadistic impulses . . . ." Fisher (1974) concludes that

> [we] have presented evidence for ongoing mental content which
> may be instrumental in triggering off the night terror. However,
> as reported here and elsewhere, night terrors may be elicited

artificially by sounding a buzzer and this constitutes the best evidence that mental activity need not be the only precipitating factor.

Tentatively the hypothesis may be advanced that episodes can be triggered by either of two different types of stimulation: (a) endogenous, in the form of ongoing mental activity during REM sleep; and (b) exogenous, in the form of loud noises or other external stimulation.

My impression is that disorders such as those considered are selectively integrated into the mechanisms of the sleep-wakefulness cycle. It would appear to me that that part of the sleep cycle classified as N-REM is significantly associated with these disorders and that the REM state is not appreciably locked into those processes. Once drowsiness or more profound states of N-REM sleep supervene, the necessary condition or conditions are met to release the disorders. Mental content probably is ongoing, whether it can be elicited or not. There appears to be a disturbance in the psychobiological state of the organism for which evidence exists throughout sleep. Acknowledged mental content certainly does not seem to be a necessary condition for the activation of these disorders. The individual's neural organization seems to be disturbed in ways that so far are largely inaccessible to our methods of study. This unfortunately leaves us favoring one interpretation over another. It is highly likely that, where the condition is extended over time, as in somnambulism or fugues, a neural state exists which present-day electroencephalography is inadequate to decipher.

I have devoted considerable space to these sleep disorders for a special reason. I am convinced that I have seen fairly frequent evidence in many patients of subtle but protracted periods of altered states of consciousness (minifugues, if you will) that do not grossly interfere with reasonable adaptation. If our knowledge of the electrophysiological processes and our techniques were adequate, I strongly suspect that very subtle shifts between vigilance and N-REM states would be recorded. Clinically the condition is not characterized by gross amnesia but by a kind of detachment that one might describe as a state of being preoccupied along with fairly plausible interpersonal engagement.

My impression is that these sleep disorders, including fugue states, are integrated into the sleep-wakefulness cycle. We do not have sufficient evidence to know what the causal patterns are, i.e., whether the fact of sleep stage or of vigilance activates the condition or is a correlate of the condition. Broughton's studies clearly show that there are physiological correlates associated with the mental state, and I believe it is reasonable to assume that this is always the case, even if methods of detection are limited. Because N-REM sleep stages cover a much wider spectrum of process temporally than does the REM state, the opportunity for a particular psychobiological activity is favored. Focal attention can be easily modified in states of mild drowsiness which need not interfere with effective living. Even the case cited by Rice and Fisher makes that quite clear.

If we assume that these fugue states may be subclinical, that an individual may function in such a way that his everyday behavior calls no attention to his patterns of living, we may still observe a kind of stereotype of thought and action in individuals in psychotherapy. Frequently, important behavioral patterns that are discussed—patterns that lead to poor solutions in living—are curiously unaffected despite painstaking exploration. The patient in therapy "understands" but is impervious. It is as if he were in a fugue. He is provoked to act out patterns of living not too dissimilar to those of individuals who wander and then return to where they started, who do not become entangled in any bizarre difficulty, but just repeat certain attitudes and modes of relating without truly grasping what they are trying to resolve. It is not infrequent that the patient has no definitive goals for treatment. What we suspect may constitute valid goals are acknowledged but are dealt with by dissociation no matter how rational the discussion.

Dissociated mental content, inaccessible to patient and therapist, must exist. I believe there is a kind of ongoing amnesia for important thought and affective experience while the therapeutic session is occurring and that the amnesia blocks the surfacing of the material. But the patient does not realize the amnesic process, and it can only be inferred by the therapist. No doubt the therapist's interest in free association is to release what is concealed within the patient's thoughts and feelings. As I stated above, I suspect that there are neurophysiological correlates that escape detection at the present time because methodology and technics are not yet sufficiently advanced and that psychotherapy is often the treatment of fugue.

REFERENCES

Arkin, A.M., Toth, M.F., Baker, J. and Haskey, J.M. (1970), The degree of concordance between content of sleep-talking and mentation recalled in wakefulness. *J. Nerv. & Ment. Dis.* 151:375–393.

Asirnsky, E., and Kleitman, N. (1953), Regularly occurring periods of eye motility and concomitant phenomena during sleep. *Science* 118: 273–274.

Broughton, R.J. (1968), Sleep Disorders: Disorders of Arousal? *Science* 159:1070–1078.

Fishbein, W. & Gutwein, B.M. (1977), Paradoxical sleep and memory storage processes. *Behav. Biol.* 19: 425–464.

Fisher, C., Kahn, E., Edwards, A., Davis, D. and Fine, J. (1974), A psycho-physiological study of nightmares and night terrors. *J. Nerv. & Ment. Dis.* 158:174–188.

Rice, E. and Fisher, C. (1976), Fugue states in sleep and wakefulness: A psychophysiological study. *J. Nerv. & Ment. Dis.* 163:79–87.

Foulkes, W.D. (1962), Dream reports from different stages of sleep. *J. Abnorm. Soc. Psychol.* 65:14–25.

Hall, C.S., Scientific American. May, 1951.

Hobson, J.A. (1975), The sleep-dream cycle: A neurobiological rhythm. In: *Pathobiology Annual.* New York: Appleton-Century-Crofts.

Kales, A. & Kales, J.P. (1974), Sleep disorders—recent findings in the diagnosis and treatment of disturbed sleep. *New Eng. J. Med.,* 290: 487–499.

Rice, E. & Fisher, C. (1976), Fugue states in sleep and wakefulness: A psychophysiological study. *J. Nerv. Ment. Dis.,* 163:79–87.

Roffwarg, H.P., Herman, J.H., Bowe-Anders, C., & Tauber, E.S. (1976), The effects of sustained alterations in sleep. The effects of sustained alterations of waking visual input. In: *The Mind in Sleep,* ed. A.A. Antrobus, Jr. & S. Ellman. New York: Lawrence Erlbaum Associates.

Roffwarg, H.P., Muzio, J.N., & Dement, W.C. (1966), Ontogenetic development of the human sleep-dream cycle. *Science,* 152:603–619.

Rojas-Ramirez, J.A. & Tauber, E.S. (1970), Paradoxical sleep in two species of avian predator (Falconiformes). *Science,* 167:1754–1755.

Tauber, E.S. (1952), Observations of counter-transference phenomena. *Samiksa, J. Indian Psychoanal.* Soc., 6:220–228.

———— (1954), Exploring the therapeutic use of counter-transference data. *Psychiatry,* 17:332–336.

———— & Green, M.R. (1959), *Prelogical Experience—an Inquiry into Dreams and other Creative Processes.* Basic Books, Inc., N.Y., 196 pp., 1959.

———— (1972), Phylogeny. In: *The Sleeping Brain,* ed. M. Chase. Los Angeles: B.I.S., University of California at Los Angeles. pp. 12–14.

———— (1974), The Phylogeny of Sleep—in *Advances in Sleep Research,* Vol. 1, Editor: E.D. Weitzman, Spectrum Publ., N.Y., 1974, pp. 133–216.

———— Coleman, R.M., & Weitzman, E.D. (1977), Electromyographic activity of non-mimetic skeletal muscles during sleep in young adults. *Annals of Neurology,* 2:66–68.

———— & Green, M.R. (1962), Color in dreams. *Amer. J. Psychother.,* 26: 221–229.

———— Handelman, G., Handelman, R., & Weitzman, E.D. (1972), Vestibular stimulation during sleep in young adults. *Arch. Neurol.*, 27: 221–228.

———— Roffwarg, H.P., & Weitzman, E.D. (1966), Eye movements and electroencephalogram activity during sleep in diurnal lizards. *Nature*, 212:1612–1613.

———— Rojas-Ramirez, J.A., & Hernandez-Peon, R. (1968), EEG and other electrophysiological correlates of wakefulness and sleep in the lizard, *Ctenosaura pectinata*. *EEG & Clin. Neurol.*, 24:424–433.

———— & Weitzman, E.D. (1969), Eye movements during behavioral inactivity in certain Bermuda reef fish. *Communications in Behav. Biol., Part A*, 3:131–135.

———— ———— Herman, J., & Pessah, M. (1973), The absence of nystagmus during REM sleep in a patient with waking nystagmus and oscillopsia. *J. Neurol., Neurosurg. Psychiat.*, 36:833–838.

6

ATTACHMENT, DETACHMENT, AND PSYCHOANALYTIC THERAPY

DAVID E. SCHECTER, M.D.

I HAVE written a series of papers on the emergence of human relatedness and the nature of human attachment.[1] "Relatedness" here refers to a relationship on the level of mental representation of self and other. "Attachment" refers to the broader ethologic term that includes pre- and postrepresentational stages. My basic premise has been that ob- servations of normal ethologic and psychic developments can con- tribute to the deepening of psychoanalytic theory and therapy. The time is now ripe for the integration of several fields of study: ethology, ego development, interpersonal and object relations, and psychoanalysis. The attachment of the human infant to its mother—and the reverse (Klaus and Kennel, 1976)—can be observed from these five points of view.

Detachment is the turning away from human relationship. This paper will briefly summarize the process of attachment in humans and will delineate the defense system of "character detachment" and its relevance to psychoanalytic theory and practice. Detachment will be described on both the ethologic and psychologic levels. *Character de- tachment* is seen as a network of defenses and coping dynamisms that become relatively stable, structuralized and chronic in the personality. *The structural network of detachment functions to protect the organism and the psyche against painful affects associated with human attachment.* In this sense character detachment can be seen as a primary and rather

---

[1] See Schecter (1968a, 1968b, 1973, 1974, 1975a, 1975b) and Schecter and Corman (1971).

awesome defense against the very process of human relatedness itself.

Detachment is neither simply "good" nor simply "bad." It can be relatively adaptive or maladaptive in relation to the individual's total psychosocial situation. Significant aspects of character detachment can be found in persons bearing every psychiatric diagnosis: in the hysteric, obsessive, depressive, in character disorders, as well as, more obviously, in the "schizoid personality" or the schizophrenic individual. Character detachment can be subjectively experienced as "never again"—as far as close human relationships are concerned. The defenses are related to persistent and usually unconscious anticipation or fear of the various forms of psychic pain. The detachment defense attempts, for example, to convert the fear of being abandoned (ego-passive fear) to an *active* movement away from relationship. The greater the depth of detachment, the greater will be the sense of futility, i.e., no hope for a "good relationship." Also, the earlier in development detachment occurs, the greater will be the potential pathologic consequences.

Detachment—as used in this paper—can be observed in any stage of development. This is in contrast to the narrower concept of "schizoid detachment" which connotes a severe and lasting detachment process between mother and child beginning in the stage of infancy. We observe detachment in varying degree when a child, adolescent, or adult suffers the loss of a beloved person. To some degree the process of mourning uses aspects of detachment as part of its repertoire. Diagnostically, it is therefore crucial to observe whether the detachment is of early origin, deep and almost total (schizoid), or whether detachment is occurring in *selective areas* in a character disorder or neurotic personality. The prognosis and therapy are obviously quite different depending on the above diagnostic criteria.

Detachment as described here may at certain times be *part of healthy coping* with a difficult situation or a certain stage of development. For example, puberty-age children almost classically go "underground," and, in varying degree, may cut off their affective relationship to their parents while they intensify their bonds to their chums. Similarly, mid-life parents, whose children are on their way out into the nonfamily world, will effectively detach themselves from certain kinds of closeness to their sons and daughters. Older-age detachment may be quite adaptive, as in a kind of Oriental detachment from an anxious "over-attachment" to life itself.

In the last section of this paper we examine the psychoanalytic situation and technique appropriate for working with character detachment. The therapeutic goal, briefly stated, is to re-establish human attachment in those areas where relatedness has been "frozen" or cut off. With "re-relatedness" in these areas, dissociated aspects of the personality—including its strengths and talents—can be reintegrated, giving rise to a situation where "activity affects" can emerge over the prior defensive stance of "embeddedness affects" (Schachtel, 1959).

We must, however, be alert to periodic and perhaps necessary regression to intrapsychic fusion or symbiotic fantasies with internal objects to fill the extreme isolation of the very detached person. We must also learn to distinguish the ensuing "pseudo independence" and the "arrogant self-sufficiency" from healthy progression toward authentic autonomy and interdependency. *The final therapeutic goal is to bring back from dissociation all the fractured, dissociated parts of the self which can then be restructured and integrated under "one roof," i.e., under the roof of the total self and under control of the ego.*

Object-relations theory has helped make respectable the empathic, real relatedness of analyst to analysand (P. Bromberg, personal communication). The model of analyst as "interpretive mirror" has been replaced by the model of participant-observation (Sullivan, 1953). Moreover, with the observation and studies of early infant-parent relationships, the analyst's empathic capacity has broadened and deepened to include preverbal and nonverbal feeling states.

ATTACHMENT AND THE CONSTANCY OF RELATIONSHIP

On the *ethologic* level of observation, an *attachment* can be defined as a unique relationship between two people that is specific and endures through time (Klaus and Kennel, 1976), though not necessarily at the level of mental representation. Attachment behaviors include fondling, kissing, cuddling, prolonged gazing—behaviors that serve both to maintain contact and exhibit affection toward a specific individual. Close attachment can persist during long separations of time and distance even though there may be at times no visible sign of its existence, indicating the infant's "memory bank" for good relationships.

On the *psychologic* level of observation, attachment is referred to here as *relatedness* which can be said to begin when the infant shows signs of *intrapsychic representation* of the bonding between infant and parent. The observational signs of this representation include the ego's anticipation of approach by mother (second month) and increasing specific preference for mother (or mother-surrogate) over less central persons in the infant's life (second to seventh month.) From the parent's side, the optimal period for bonding and attachment is seen to occur *immediately after birth*. Moreover, Klaus and Kennel (1976) note that premature infants who have been separated from parents show a significantly higher incidence of child battering, due in part to a failure of infant bonding. Those premature infants who were handled from birth onward by their parents thrived better and were less battered— to a significant extent—than preemies who were separated from their parents while in the hospital. These important discoveries also indicate that the parents who watch the birth of their children and handle them from birth onward are more likely to develop a specific attachment to the infant.

The process of attachment (ethologic) and the state of related-ness (psychologic) are central features of the human condition. The infant, though active, is too helpless to survive on his own. Both par-ents and infant are equipped with biologic and culturally given modes of forming a lasting bond, a bond from which all other bonds are, in part, derived. This statement applies equally to the formation of self-identity. The particular stages of formation of this bond to the level of "object constancy" have been described in detail elsewhere (Schecter, 1973, 1974). Suffice it to repeat here that the process is not based primarily on need tension-reduction. Rather is the forma-tion of the bond organized around an evolution of bipersonal inter-actions where tension rises and falls in rhythmic fashion. This evolution is true for mutual smiling, eye-to-eye "choreography" (Stern, 1971), and playful interaction, including peek-a-boo (Schecter, 1973). *These processes require an interpersonal model* quite different from, for ex-ample, the reduction of oral drive tension.

In 1968, as part of a paper (Schecter 1973) delivered at the twenty-fifth anniversary symposium of the William Alanson White Institute, I put forth several hypotheses concerning human development that were based on direct observations in natural family settings. I will summarize these briefly.

1. Social stimulation and reciprocal interaction, often playful and not necessarily "drive"-connected or tension-reducing constitute a basis for the development of specific social attachments and relation-ships between the infant and others.

2. We see in early reciprocal stimulation and response the pre-cursors to *all* human communication, including eventual courtship pat-terns (the "invitation to dance").

3. Without adequate social stimulation, as is found in institutional infants (Provence and Lipton, 1952), deficits develop in emotional

and social relationships, language, abstract thinking, and inner controls. These ego functions and structures constitute the building blocks of human development and are necessary precursors to moral development and social collaboration which, in turn, constitute the fabric of our society. *It is safe to predict that until "society" and its responsible institutions take care of the needs of its infants, children and adults, it will suffer ongoing generational family and social disorganization.*[2]

Stages of Development of the Capacity for Constancy of Relatedness[3]

1. *Undifferentiated stage*: Experience is not located "inside" or "outside" a self. Mother and infant form a symbiotic unit. Experience only begins to be defined as "psychologic" at stage 2.

2. *Beginning differentiation*:

a. *A dawning self and other (mother)*: There is still enough fluidity of organization for the infant's experience to oscillate between more and less differentiated states. This period overlaps the symbiotic and early separation-individuation stages (Mahler, Pine and Bergman, 1975). If the oscillation is too rapid or too extreme the child will be forced to use detachment defenses against the disorienting, anxiety-inducing affects of oscillation.

b. *Experience becomes organized affectively and cognitively as "good" and "bad."* These experiences precede the more differentiated experience of good-me, good-mother, etc.

3. *Further differentiation into*: (a) good-me, (b) bad-me, (c) good-mother, (d) bad-mother, (e) good relationship, (f) bad relationships. These further differentiations occur during the phases of separation-individuation. These gestalten are referred to as *personifications* by Sullivan (1953) and as *mental representations* in classic psychoanalysis.

---

[2] A number of observers, including Bowlby (1973) and Heinicke and Westheimer (1965), have studied the longer-term effects of separation and have shown that affects such as hopelessness and a sense of futility follow upon prolonged separation, especially with poor substitute care. Bowlby (1973) also cites a number of studies in which a surprisingly high percentage of parents—from 27 to 50 per cent—*admit* to threats of abandonment as a way of controlling or punishing a child. If to this we add more subtle abandonment or withdrawal-type of parental behavior, we see that *it is likely that a majority of children in our society realistically experience the threat of abandonment.*

[3] A somewhat parallel scheme is presented by Kernberg (1976).

4. The above state of affairs (2b and 3) can be described as the *normal developmental base* for the later defense mechanism of *splitting,* e.g., "mostly-good" vs. "mostly-bad mother"; "good relation" vs. "bad relation."

5. During the second and third year of life, the splits ("good" and "bad" self and mother) become integrated in their unitary wholeness in varying degrees. Mother (good-or-bad) is then *"my mother."* Self (good-or-bad) is to a great extent *"my self."* Relationship (good-or-bad) is now *"me-and-(m)other."* No longer are there simply categories of good and bad experience; rather, various levels of complexity of affect and mental representations interweave with internal and external object-persons.

6. The child not only discriminates and values his mother selectively, but also begins to represent her mentally with *qualities of increasing permanence and objectivity.* Even in the face of cruelty or frustration, or during a limited absence, the mother continues to be preferred and central to the child's life. *This centrality constitutes the achievement of "constancy of relationship" which implies "object-person constancy" as well as a growing sense of continuity and sameness in the self ("self-constancy.")*

The relationship is now represented mentally (intrapsychically), invested with intense affect, and develops growing stability over the years. We tend to think that there is a "critical"—or at least, "optimal"— period for such *constancy of relationship* to be defined and maintained with growing stability and an increasing number of persons (during the second and third years and onwards). Mental health is predicated on these developments, which pertain to parent as well as child. *The warps and deficits in ego and interpersonal development derive in large part from a failure to achieve a level of constancy of relationship with one or more persons early in life.*

All of the above develops in the context of increasing separation-individuation, of growing ego autonomy, and of re-relatedness on a more allocentric (Schachtel, 1959) and decreasing egocentric basis (Piaget, 1954).

The work of individual development and of therapy consists of *integrating the polar splits* of good and bad mother into the felt concept "my mother." As Sullivan suggests, the learning of language and its word symbol "mother" facilitates, and in part coerces, the integration of the good and bad polarities of experience. *The further task of both development and therapy is to be able to endure and maintain the constancy* (continuity and sameness) of the relationship, of the self

(self-identity), and of the object (object constancy) despite the prevalence of ambivalent affects toward mother. *Constancy of relatedness can be defined in part as the capacity to maintain the integrated relationship (internal) to the mother in the face of the conflicting affects such as love and hate.*[4] The love object will not be exchanged and is not interchangeable even under conditions of severe cruelty.

The development of constancy of relationship is only begun in infancy. It is still highly unstable in early childhood.[5] It is really a *lifelong developmental task* to retain and modify the above described constancy under the vicissitudes of separation-individuation and of ambivalent feelings. A fresh or sharp loss or disappointment threatens to test the stability of constancy, and, clinically, we then find the splitting of parent or spouse, and/or of self into "all good" and "all bad."[6] The same is true of "the relationship" which remains potentially split into good or bad. Fairbairn (1952) describes in great detail how a splitting of the object-person is related to the splitting of the ego into (a) the "internal saboteur" and (b) the "libidinal ego"—splits from (c) the "central ego." Though each of these is interdependent, they achieve some degree of autonomy and can have separate lines of development. In Sullivan's language, the "good" and "bad" parts of the self becomes split off, that is, dissociated from the unity of the whole personality. In analytic therapy of deeply detached persons, a spontaneous desire develops for the various compartments of the self to be under "one roof" whose subjective expression includes "my self" or "all me." Some patients have described wanting the self "inside" instead of somewhere "outside"—a condition in which character defenses had been "inside" and false self-defenses had been experienced as the "outside" or "social" self. At this point in analysis there is a sense of momentous change and often a sense of "new beginning" (Balint, 1953). In my own work I have found this "new beginning" phenomenon occurs when the good me and the loving superego begin to predominate over the bad me and the condemning superego.

The clinical relevance of the concept of constancy of relationship is enormous. To the extent this capacity has been developed in a stable

---

[4] Burgner and Edgcumbe (1972) arrive at a parallel concept, the *"capacity for constant relationships"* as it develops from the more primitive *need-satisfying relationship.*

[5] See Pine (1974) on the subject of stability and liability of object constancy.

[6] This would be considered "defensive splitting" in contrast to the normal polarization into "good" and "bad" experiences. See Freud's (1938) paper on splitting of the ego.

way, there will be less tendency to splitting of the object-person or of the self into all good or all bad—tendencies seen in the borderline character and in paranoid and schizophrenic persons. Moreover, such constancy anchors and centers the self during its process of separation-individuation, thereby leading to increased ego autonomy and to less tendency to regression to fusion states when under stress. Also, constancy of relation protects against a sense of total loss or abandonment (e.g., when this occurs in reality with the external object) since *the internal constant relationship, if strong enough, will help mourn the loss of the external object-person.*

DETACHMENT

Having described in a general way the process of human attachment, let us turn our attention to the process of detachment. Detachment in the *ethologic* sense refers to patterns of movement away from attachment. In the *psychic* sense, detachment connotes a defense against relationship *on the level of mental representation.* Detachment can be adaptive or maladaptive depending on the total psychic situation.

Detachment has been defined as a network of defenses whose function is to undermine or sever the process of attachment in order to avoid or reduce psychic pain that is attendant on a state of relatedness. It is an attempt to anesthetize psychic pain. Detachment implies a "never again" or an "I don't care" affect as far as one's relation to specifically loved persons.[7] It attempts to neutralize the anxieties that accompany relationships, e.g., the anxiety of separation, of abandonment, of the stranger, of loss of love, or of yearning but without hope.

Detachment in its broadest sense has a biological base in development. Sullivan (1953) describes the phenomenon of "somnolent detachment" in the infant when he is overly anxious or overstimulated, as in pain. The infant's biologic defenses include both falling asleep and visual aversion, literally a turning away from a source of anxiety, e.g., the angry mother. These biologic mechanisms are seen here as the *anlagen to the psychic defense of detachment.*

My own interest in defensive detachment derives from Bowlby's (1973) description of the young child's separation reactions. Bowlby used the term "detachment" to describe the third stage of a two-year-

---

[7] There is a lovely children's book (age five to seven) by Maurice Sendak (1962) about Pierre who "didn't care" until he was swallowed by a lion at which point he "cared."

old's reaction upon physical separation from the mother due to the child's hospitalization. After the initial stages of stormy, *angry protest* followed by *despair* (sadness, regression, loss of interest in the environment), a third stage—*detachment*—was characterized by "improved spirit" albeit with an *active avoidance of mother or by a distinct "cooling"* of the strong specific attachment behavior usually shown at this age toward the mother. Other sequelae may appear as well, such as anxious clinging, sometimes mixed with aggressive detachment, serious negativism and oppositionalism may become dominant in the character (Bowlby, 1973, p. 225).

The detached child was described as committing herself less and less to succeeding figures and becoming more self-centered and more preoccupied with need satisfaction, e.g., desiring sweets and material things. The parallel—phenomenologically and etiologically—between the direct observation (by camera) of Bowlby's detachment phase following actual separation and characterologic detachment in adults is quite striking. Here I am suggesting in effect that adult detachment is a homologue to child detachment. It has occurred to me that Bowlby's description of the detachment phase needs to be understood as a process that may be conceptualized on two levels: (1) the behavioral ethologic level (pre- and postrepresentational) and (2) as intrapsychic defense.

Bowlby (1973) has observed that detachment from a parent is more frequent in relation to mother than to father and that the duration of the child's detachment correlates highly with the length of his separation. Upon reunion, mothers complained that they were treated as strangers for the first few days. The separated children were afraid to be left alone and were far more clinging than they had been before the separation. Bowlby believes that after very long or repeated separations, detachment can persist indefinitely. *It is this aspect of detachment that I have used in my concept of character detachment.* It is true both in Bowlby's children and in partially detached characters that detachment can alternate with intense symbiosislike clinging and/or intensely ambivalent attitudes including being rejecting, hostile, or defiant toward mother. There remains of course a lingering fear in the child—and later in the adult—that he will suffer new separations should he make any new attachments. Moreover, in the attempt to make new attachments, he brings his detachment defenses with him in a way that resists that attachment process itself.

I see the intrapsychic detachment defense becoming available to the child not only after real physical separations but, on another level, ensuing upon the realization of a greater sense of psychic separateness during the separation-individuation processes in childhood and in later stages of development. Mahler, Pine, and Bergman (1975) describe a change of affect of a depressive tone that comes over the child (around 18 months) when he becomes more aware of the separateness of his experience from that of his mother. This dawning realization—during the second year of life—can be seen as the developmental anlage to the later phenomenon of existential aloneness.

It is in the process of detachment and normal separation-individuation that the internal capacity for constancy of relationship becomes most critical. The more stable the constancy and the deeper the structure of the loving superego, the less traumatic will be the separation anxiety and the ensuing detachment defense.[8] In a sense we can say that a firm, healthy constancy of relationship in some degree immunizes child and adult reactions to loss, separation, and abandonment. If a good relationship is internalized in my self, I will be able to endure separation and loss without the need for extreme "schizoid-like" detachment. I will also be helped to mourn aspects of the primary relationship that are being lost, such as omnipotence and symbiosis.

Character Detachment and Schizoid Personality

We may now inquire into the similarities and differences between *character detachment* and the *schizoid personality*. Both to some degree may have in common the following traits described by Guntrip (1968) as "schizoid": withdrawnness, introversion, self-sufficiency, narcissism, loss of affect, loneliness, depersonalization and/or derealization, regression, and a sense of superiority (often secret). My observations in psychoanalytic practice and supervision have made clear to me that when the analysis goes deeply enough, many patients who, in psychiatric diagnostic terms, present themselves as hysteric, obsessional, or depressive character disorders are suffering as well from characterologic detachment. Some schools of thought refer to this area of depth as the basic "schizoid position" (Fairbairn, 1952) or "schizoid state" (Guntrip, 1968), but the etiologic assumption of these two views is that the patient experiences his deep craving for love as destructive (Guntrip, 1968, pp 29–31, 102). This *can* be true, but it should be

---

[8] Defenses cannot full regulate the ego, but they can predominate in a way that does not allow the embattled ego to gain new input and energy from its interpersonal relations. With defenses predominating, the other ego functions are not available, e.g., for object relations (internal and external).

kept entirely open as to whether it is *the* primary etiologic factor. This ultimate "position" smacks too much of original sin, much as does the Kleinian assumption of a primal oral destructive force—derived from the death instinct—in the three-month-old infant. Whether these basic assumptions of what amount to "evil" impulses are ascribed to a three-month-old infant or to a mother, our theory is led away from scientific observation—including interactional cognitive-affective ego development—and back to adultomorphic-blame psychologies. By staying with the concept of "character detachment," we leave open for further study how and when the future patient gets into this awesome position of having to ward off meaningful human attachment.

It is of interest here that Sullivan's notion of "malevolent transformation" implies character detachment, and is an "open system" concept, since it does not make any assumptions about "ultimate evil." Rather, the concept addresses itself to the operational defensive function of this transformation in which there is anticipation of rebuff of the need for tenderness. Like detachment, the malevolent transformation can be found in all kinds of psychiatric diagnoses, though the extreme paranoid may reveal this dynamism in "pure culture."

Unlike the concept "schizoid position," the detachment defenses can arise and be used at *any* stage of the life cycle, and affect the personality in highly varying degrees. Naturally the earlier and more severe the etiologic trauma and psychic pain, the more severe and deep the character detachment will be—and in this instance the more it will resemble the schizoid position with its massive and permanent dissociation of large parts of the personality from a very early stage of development. Put yet another way: to the extent that detachment is predominant in the character organization, the resulting structure may approach the appearance of the so-called schizoid character. The latter usually implies a lack of capacity for intimate relatedness. A varying degree of character detachment, on the other hand, is seen in persons who are quite capable of intimate relationships.

Detachment may be observed on a number of levels and uses varying combinations of defense mechanisms: (1) stoppage of "affect flow" interpersonally and intrapsychically (*repression*):[9] (2) *isolation* of affect from idea; (3) *denial* of attachment, i.e., a disavowal of an attachment; (4) *splitting* of the internal object-person and of the ego.

---

[9] When detachment is prominent, the affects may still be discovered as flowing between split-off dissociated parts of the self and internal object-persons, e.g., internal persecution of the "bad me" by the "internal saboteur" or "condemning superego."

Under certain optimal conditions, including a trusting psycho-analytic situation, persons with character detachment are able to develop a richness of affective responsiveness, a capacity for affective flow inter- and intrapersonally, and the capacity for constancy of relatedness, including self- and object constancy. The schizoid character, in contrast, is in part defined by his severe limitation in or lack of capacity for full "relationship constancy" (Horner, 1975). Characters with strong detachment defenses may use these defenses to "shut down" relatedness or to renunciate object relations. However, their potential for and history of relatively full relatedness can be established diagnostically—in contrast to what is usually implied by the term "schizoid character."

Character detachment may be structurally discernible in certain "pockets of resistance" to relatedness. With analysis "re-relatedness" can be established in those areas associated with danger or threat. The rest of the personality may be fairly healthy and available for the analytic process and relationship. The "schizoid hollowness" is not necessarily present in someone who, nevertheless, has significant detachment defenses. Behind these defenses one often finds a strong desire to come out of those frozen-off areas of detachment (the need-fear dilemma). For the schizoid character, the experience of *affects-in-relationship* is associated with extreme psychic pain and is often ego-alien. Severe schizoid character, almost by definition, implies such a global threat to any kind of intimate relatedness that the prognosis is guarded as far as the therapeutic possibility for ego reorganization and positive growth of structures to the extent they are inherently lacking (ego deficits). For example, the structure of *relationship constancy* would have literally to be "grown" (by internalizations) in long, intensive, trusting psychoanalytic therapy.

I have seen a considerable number of persons who have lost a parent in childhood or adolescence. Many of these have defended against the painful affect of personal object loss via *partial detachment that may on the surface mimic schizoid withdrawal*. There is a danger that the presenting picture will mistakenly be diagnosed as schizoid. This would constitute a serious misdiagnosis since the prognostic course and treatment of choice would lead to a plan of treatment ill-suited to one whose detachment is in part an *unsuccessful attempt at mourning*.[10] Children and adolescents who have lost a parent will in fact present a combination of both (1) a detachment from potential

---

[10]It is most difficult for children and adolescents (and even adults) to do the work of mourning. See Martha Wolfenstein's (1966) "How is Mourning Possible?"

painful affect associated with loss and (2) denial of the parent's death. If the latter denial were total and absolute, there would be no pain of loss. The need on the child's part for defensive detachment indicates that the denial of death is only partially effective.

Both in the schizoid personality and severe character detachment, "broken" parts of the self remain to function on their own. With reattachment, these parts of the self are rebuilt into a central self which gains increasing energy from the reverberating circuits that ensue in interpersonal relationships. "Broken" parts of the self are both the source and result of great anxiety and are, so to speak, looking for a central self and ego with which to become one (as in "getting it together").

PSYCHOANALYTIC THERAPY OF CHARACTER DETACHMENT

As mentioned above, our main goal in psychoanalytic therapy is to re-establish attachment with the patient in those detached areas that are frozen or cut off. As in all psychoanalytic therapy, we look to the healthy, nondetached areas to make a therapeutic alliance with the analysand. The alliance is largely based on the hope of relieving psychic pain through the therapeutic relationship, and the shared capacity for both therapist and patient to *look together* with their observing egos at the whole person of the patient, including his interactions with the analyst and others. The analyst has the added work of keeping in touch with and analyzing his own countertransference. The latter reactions may include a sense of being drained or strained by the patient's resistance, especially in his areas of detachment. In brief, we use the patient's strengths, curiosity, and pain to set up rapport and a working alliance.

The analysand needs the therapist to be emotionally available from the beginning phase of the analysis when some detached persons may be experienced as arid, obsessional, and intellectualized in style. The analyst's attitude should be one of watchful waiting with a mobility to move in and make connections for the patient so that he can begin to see what he feels or might have felt if his detachment had not been so complete in a given area.

I am reminded of a 27-year-old patient I saw some time ago. Mr. M.'s chief complaints were chronic tension and sleepwalking. Mr. M. developed a strong loyalty to his "analytic sessions" without being able to say or feel that he was becoming attached to his analyst. Gradually, by encouraging him to talk about those experiences in which he did feel some emotion, we developed a bond of shared experience. He became expressive concerning his tastes for food, music, his boss—but almost nothing in relation to his wife. On the one hand, he indicated an attitude to his wife of "never again shall I become attached," but, on the other hand, he betrayed a quiet fondness for his wife who was sensitive to his boundaries and his need for "psychic space."

After some months of analysis I inquired about his first masturbation fantasies. He described how he had simply imaged a penis all by itself, unattached to any person. This extreme detachment in the sexual-emotional-interpersonal area led us into his extreme sense of isolation in childhood and adolescence. The penis fantasy remained detached from persons even after he met his wife. She was a nurse, seductive and warm, but in a way that was not threateningly intrusive. Gradually, as the therapy and the relation to his wife progressed simultaneously, the masturbation symbol of the lonely penis gave way to direct feelings of love toward his wife. This process occurred over a period of three years during which there was careful inquiry into the various threats that he experienced to any close attachment.

In the first year of analysis he retrieved a memory that was rather striking to both of us. The memory was of himself as a toddler, entrapped in a wire-mesh cage that had been placed over his bed each night when he was "put to sleep." The rationale for the use of the cage had been to prevent him from wandering and thus keep him safe. During our "looking together" at this two-year-old boy in him he became enraged at the inhumanity of his parents' attempt to control and imprison him, albeit for "his own good." This memory, now recovered with the affects of rage and of fear of being entrapped, helped us to unlock the mystery of his sleepwalking which stopped shortly after the exploration of this memory. His sleepwalking had begun around four years of age and stopped in the second year of the analysis. From the analysis of his current as well as past sleepwalking it became clear that he was searching while asleep to make contact with his parents, both of whom were cool, detached people. He had wanted especially to reach his mother. Following this insight he allowed himself to move much closer to his wife affectionately and sexually. The patient ascertained from his mother that the cage was removed after age four and that his sleepwalking began *after* that time. There was no evidence for sexual curiosity as a motive for the somnambulism.

The analytic inquiry was made in the spirit of an alliance, trying to understand and relive in the transference his deep yearning for contact, especially holding and being held. These latter two modalities were actualized with his wife, while in his analysis he described a feeling of "being held" by the analyst who had "faith" that he was not the robotlike, controlled, efficient person that he presented to the world. Later in the analysis the patient was able to express a sense of loyalty and gratitude to "the analysis" although he still staved off direct expression of feeling for the analyst. These warm feelings were brought into his marriage where intercourse, stroking, embracing, and verbalization of love became more natural for him.

In our reconstruction of his early years—partly based on his mother's information—it became clear that he had received a warm, facilitating environment during his infancy but was *restrained*—physically and emotionally—*from the exuberance of his toddler days*. The patient had felt that this had been the situation even before it was corroborated by his mother and that as a caged child he had vowed to "never again" trust someone who might be loving. The "reattachment" through his analysis and through his relationship to his wife was complete enough for him to establish "relationship constancy" with both his wife and his analyst, and later as a father to his children. Retrospectively, one of the key factors on the analyst's part was a conviction that this man had the silent "growth buds" for an intimate relation. The main signs for this included the highly intense investment he made to the analysis from early on. I have learned that commitment to the analysis is more accurate prognostically than the analysand's verbalized attachment behavior to the analyst.

I have had many patients who similarly felt emotionally imprisoned and unable to contact their loving and joyful feelings. The therapeutic position I have taken is one of offering myself as a witness from an optimal distance—so that I will neither inappropriately intrude on the self-membrane nor fail to be available if and when the patient is able to make contact. The content of the interpretations has to be sufficiently accurate so that the patient can feel he is in a true "holding" (Winnicott, 1965) environment.

In my experience it is crucial to refrain from making comments that will predictably increase the resistance. The attitude of both analyst and analysand is one of "hovering" (Freud) or "bare" attention (Nyanaponika, 1973). We notice that the resistance centers around issues whose conscious awareness will bring pain. These issues usually have as their central affects anxiety and fear or depression, but also, potentially, great *shame and humiliation.* Raw shame is one of the most potent dissociating forces largely *because it threatens to suddenly lower self-esteem and annihilate the very "sense of self."* Hence the aphorism: "There is no problem so great as the shame of it."

The therapeutic principle of *looking together* and sharing experience has its roots in the mother-infant relationship from the second half of the first year onward. The paradigm consists of the infant's focusing on some spectacle by gazing at or pointing to it, and the mother's responding in some sensitive way to the infant's communication.

In observational studies conducted with children and parents in their natural setting, it has been most impressive to see the intensity of affect—and the amount of "free time"—experienced by parent and child.[11] The affect can be described for the most part as joyful "activity affect"(Schachtel, 1959) and has the quality of being peremptory, and *exclusively* oriented to parent and child. In several families, the fathers complained openly about feeling excluded from this private experience of mother and child, an experience that has the quality of an *exclusively shared private mythology.* A whole body of play, fantasy, and reality becomes interwoven into a system fully known—usually—to one parent and child. *Psychoanalytic therapy is, in part, also a shared mythology* in which the objective truth of the content is secondary to the peremptoriness of its being experienced as mutual, and close to the *subjective sense of truth about one's experience.* Edgar Levenson (1978) has described the psychoanalytic process as one that does not rely only on the truth of the professed content. "Nor does it depend on the therapist's participation with the patient, but rather on a dialectic interaction of these elements." "It is this dialectic between understanding and newness which makes for the core of therapeutic discourse. Metaphor is independent of time and space. It is always true."

The melting down, through analysis, of the sense of shame and its cover-ups allows both analyst and analysand to look at areas that have been dissociated by detachment as these areas surface through dreams, fantasies, marginal thoughts, and nonobsessional free association. If this new body of experience is not foreclosed by interpretation and "explanation," then *"interpretive pointing"* may be used to enhance the special sense of the therapeutic dyad looking together, as in snor-

---

[11] Studies in Ego Development at Albert Einstein College of Medicine, Grant # H D 01155–01, National Institute of Child Health and Human Development.

keling, in subterranean waters. Interpretation and explanation may falsely "wrap up" a dream, for example, before the dream and its associations are afforded an "open state" where it is possible to come back again and again to the dream from new perspectives, and even to redream familiar dreams with new endings. *The therapeutic attitude, then, is one of curiosity and exploration rather than explanation and interpretation.* Explanation and interpretation are often used as "cere-bralized" counterresistance—a distancing by the analyst who is threatened by the necessary but finely titrated process of reattachment to a partially detached or "schizoid" person.

What I have noted here about sharing pathways to unconscious material using images and meanings in fantasy and dreams also applies to the exploration of the analysand's "realities" and history—indeed because *it is "his-story," the one and only story he has, one that gives a sense of orientation, identity, time continuity, and drama to his own life.* For myself, if only to keep most hours interesting, I need to have some sense of drama, and of history in its alive current and largely intrapsychic sense. The *analytic expectation* is to share experience in depth, and so our attitude in analytic therapy should strongly project this expectation; otherwise analyst and patient are doing something else with each other and that had best be explored.

It is uncanny how in a good analytic relationship both analyst and analysand find the right "spot" to occupy in the dimensions of closeness vs. distance and attachment vs. detachment.[12] We know intuitively not to move in too quickly, or too intimately, with a suspicious person. For the patient, at first the analyst can be felt as someone who is dangerous, someone who may seduce or disarm a hard-won but extremely isolated fortress of pseudo autonomy. Nevertheless, the patient has come to us for help so that we have the right to inquire into his expectations, his needs, his fears, his shame, his ideal wishes—but always with a sense of what his defensive system can bear. A common question I ask of a depressed or withdrawn patient is when he last felt good or hopeful. Not infrequently, as our contact breaks through

---

[12] "A company of porcupines crowded themselves very close together one cold winter's day so as to profit by one another's warmth, and to save themselves from being frozen to death. But soon they felt one another's quills which induced them to separate again. And now when the need for warmth brought them nearer together, again the second evil arose once more. So that they were driven backwards and forwards from one trouble to the other until they discovered a safe distance at which they could more tolerably exist" (Schopenhauer).

the detachment area via the transference and/or the "real relationship," he may respond with a choked-up feeling or with the shedding
of some as yet undifferentiated tears.[13] If this human contact is felt as
too threatening, the following analytic session is often distinctly cooler,
more distanced, or may even be cancelled.

Each participant in the analytic work becomes familiar with the
"psychic space" around the self-boundary (ego boundary; Federn
[1952]) and then with the boundary itself. The latter is more accurately experienced as a "membrane-around-the-self," a membrane which
is semipermeably selective; certain affects and information can flow
"in" and "out" in relation to given interpersonal situations. The concepts "self-membrane" and of a membrane around compartments
within the self are too complex to discuss in detail in this paper.[14]
Suffice it to say that analytic therapy works toward an optimal permeability of such membranes to facilitate the flow of information and
affects.

The many therapeutic issues associated with character detachment tend to emerge naturally from an understanding of the phenom-
enology of attachment and detachment. For example, in the observation
of infants and children, one has the experience of being responded
to as the "bad stranger" whose presence can evoke near-panic in the
six-month-old infant. Analysts who have observed attachment-separa-
tion stress behaviors in children are less likely to respond with counterresistance when these affects are expressed in the adult analytic situation.
Similarly, the capacity for empathy with the more primitive nonverbal
affects may be more available in analysts who have had experience
with infants and children. When one has seen "in the raw" the deep
shame, humiliation, and rages of the preschooler, it is easier to recognize
the "cover-up" of such affects in adults—a cover-up to protect the
patient from a mortification of self-esteem.[15]

In my work with adults, I use both developmental diagnosis[16] and
"developmental therapy" with a particular interest in what ego strengths

---

13 An important task of the therapy is the analysand's *learning a well-differ-
entiated vocabulary for his often undifferentiated emotions.* The therapist may
sometimes have to offer the vocabulary and the metaphors, as in a "Chinese menu."

14 See Landis (1970) and Federn (1952) for a searching view of these issues.

15 In the process of "growing up," disidentification and the mourning of
diminishing identifications with parents can stimulate feelings of shame and dis-
loyalty.

16 See Anna Freud (1965), Negera (1966), Kernberg (1976), and Horner
(1975).

can be engaged for the patient's potential growth in therapy. An example of developmental therapy is seen in the long analysis required to build a "capacity for constancy in relationship." In deprivation or cumulative trauma (Khan, 1974) of infancy and childhood, a capacity for constancy has failed to develop or, if it has developed, it remains highly unstable in relation to the ordinary stresses of life. *The building of a stable constancy of relatedness with the analyst* may require many years with an up and down, "in and out" relationship (Guntrip, 1968). During this long haul, the analyst is tested many times—especially as to his trustworthiness. Each time the patient comes closer to "surrendering" to trust there tends to be a largely fabricated "paranoid attack" which then justifies the patient's moving back to his pretrust and preconstancy position. "Good" and "bad" become all-or-none categories again as is seen in the borderline personality (Kernberg, 1976).

We should not allow the presenting behavioral facade to determine our judgment of the "shape" of a character structure. In both practice and supervision I have seen patients who initially present as shy, inhibited, withdrawn "schizoid" persons turn out to have a rich inner life and capacity for change in analysis. I personally need to find some evidence of "psychic growth buds" that will be available for development in analysis before making the serious commitment to an analytic treatment project.

Two of the psychic strengths I refer to are: (1) a self-observing ego; and (2) a capacity to look, to see, to portray and share—by words, dreams, associations, and through the transference—the nature of the patient's "inner psychic world" (Sandler and Rosenblatt, 1962). Obviously many of the therapeutic suggestions presented here apply not only to issues of character detachment but to psychoanalytic work in general.

How one separates or detaches (these are different) is *the* crucial factor to the next stage of interpersonal development. If one has left—or detached—with an inner sense of badness, one brings this "badness" from one situation to another. This phenomenon is seen clearly in the "transferences" from early (original) family life to marital relations or to transference in the narrower technical sense in the analytic situation itself. One brings one's badness and tries to convert the analysis into a "bad relationship." Against this, the forces of the "good-me" and "loving superego" and whatever available "constancy of good relationship" there is all act to facilitate the ongoing analysis in which the analyst "refuses" to treat the patient as if he were "really bad." In effect, the analyst does not follow the patient's attempt to "spoil" the relationship and thus challenges the patient's sense of omnipotent malevolence—a complex that may have resulted from extreme dissociation and detachment in earlier years.

Detachment also functions to protect a frequently hard-won and still fragile *sense of ego autonomy.* This defensive stance needs to be explored in depth and with care, since the patient's behavior may present itself as "perversely oppositional," defiant, negativistic, or "wanting to control the therapy" *much as he is used to control attachment vs. detachment and the flow of his affective life.* To surrender some control of the therapy may feel like a total surrender of autonomy of the self unless this stage of development has gone far enough in its integration with basic trust. The analysand is often found to be hypersensitive to having his "membrane" invaded by "interpretation," "explanation" from "outside," or even worse, from a superior posture. Thus, psychoanalytic therapy with character detachment involves: (1) validating the patient's attempt to preserve his not-yet-solid autonomy, and (2) clarifying with the patient how in almost every important life relationship he suffers now from feeling imprisoned by the protective fortress he has built to control relationships. The temptation toward regressive resymbiosis and refusion, *may,* in some cases, be therapeutically warranted on a transitional basis, but must be monitored very carefully. Almost every patient with whom I have worked eventually describes the experience of the "fortress," "prison," or "shell" in association with a "lack of connection" to another person, a lonely or isolated state, a lack of nourishment interpersonally—all with an underlying sense of deep futility.

At this greater depth, we observe clinically that a kind of somnolence, a deadening, heavy tone sets in, sometimes in relation to all experience, sometimes selectively, as in Bowlby's case of two-and-a-half-year-old Laura where the detachment was in relation to the separation from mother, the person to whom she had been most specifically attached. In separations from or loss of a beloved person (or part of the self), we see that the partially adaptive function of detachment is to maintain the homeostasis in varying degree and *protect the self from being flooded by painful affect.* It is as if the psyche has the capacity to form or differentiate out a "membrane" to protect the self. In situations of impending danger or of loss (actual or sensed), the hypothetical membrane becomes almost nonpermeable, in effect like the so-called schizoid shell, thus cutting off the input or conscious registration or expression of those affects that are still preconsciously available within the membrane. In contrast to catharsis, the increased but selective permeability of the membrane (structural change) and the flow of affects constitute one of the principal goals of psychoanalysis.

It is in this area of affect flow that it is most tempting to hypothecate a sensitively and selectively permeable "membrane-around-the-self." The "membrane" is, in part, our imaginary construct, but also an expression of a subjectively felt experience. We will thus forego the temptation to describe this membrane as if we could see it through a microscope. Yet at this point further work on the concept of ego or self-boundary and membrane may be useful in a heuristic sense. Certainly, our experiential language almost takes it for granted, e.g., "he's getting under my skin," or "she's coming through to me"—indicating a barrier or "membrane" that an affect must get "through."

Our language is replete with expressions referring to a person as "hardened" rather than "tender" in relation to certain affects—for example, "hard-nosed" or "hard-hearted" vs. "tender" or "bleeding-heart." These expressions involve a number of functions related but not identical to each other, such as the capacity (1) to *empathize,* (2) to *identify* partially with another, or (3) to be *contaged* by the other's affect. Though each of these phenomena is significantly different, they have one aspect in common—the "permeability" of the "membrane-around-the self." Without sufficient permeability we suffer excessive detachment—a possible advantage if this detachment is selective to negative affects such as a flooding of anxiety from another person. However, in general, all depends on the total personal situation and context, and the balance between attachment and detachment. If I am characteristically "hard-hearted" to a person in need and never allow him partially and temporarily to "get into me," then I will not make a good analyst, friend, or parent. On the other hand, if every child or patient's anxiety or disappointment becomes "mine" in too great a degree and for too long a time, I will be flooded, "overidentified," and rendered helpless to be a psychoanalyst, or to be helpful in any other way—especially to the extent that the patient and I have become totally the same. The art of living, then, depends on a subtle set of regulatory ego functions which feed back to the self signals of how that self is coping with what has been "taken in" and expressed out" in the way of information, including its affective charge.

Psychoanalytic therapy aims to explore and increase the awareness of the patient and therapist *especially in the areas of needs and fears.* The need-fear dilemma is not specific to schizophrenia: in some degree it is a universal human problem. If we gradually work into the depth of the patient's defensive structures, we discover that he is a being who *needs* despite the awesome defensive "antineed" detachment structures that have become so synonymous with his very identity. For this reason, to work analytically at this level requires great patience and endurance since the therapeutic alliance is involved in nothing less than a restructuring of the self-identity. Self-consciousness, shame, humiliation, and pride will be the analyst's guides to uncovering hidden and dangerously experienced needs and affects—often associated disparagingly with being childish or babyish.

Authoritarian approaches in analysis—some of which may constitute an induced countertransference response to the patient's withholding—may result in a greater resistance in the form of an obvious "clam-closing-its-shell" reaction, or, even more dangerously, by *pseudo compliance* to an often unconscious sadistic intervention on the part of the therapist. The ego protects the self by responding with the unconscious attitude: "I will get you off my back and at a greater distance by appearing to fulfill the goals you expect of me." This attitude becomes fused with what has been called the "negative therapeutic reaction" since *the patient must now cling to self-sufficiency as his personal sign of autonomy and continuity of the self.* He may go to the extreme of suicide to defend a fragile autonomy. The analyst must be most sensitive to the patient's inner struggle between a temptation to fuse symbiotically with the therapist at the one extreme, or to keep him out altogether in his struggle for a sense of prideful autonomy. *When patient and analyst realize in depth that this is part of the continuing human struggle between the polarities of symbiosis and individuation, a greater compassion and a melting away of the humiliation may result.*

As in most psychoanalytic papers, the emphasis here has been on the psychopathologic aspects of detachment. I must reiterate, however, that there are potentially *healthy* aspects of defenses and coping mechanisms involving detachment in the service of developmental progression and differentiation. Especially when we take into account individual differences in sensitivity thresholds and the dizzying amount of input from an urban environment, we realize that *the issue is one of balance whenever the polarities of attachment and detachment have to be reconciled and integrated.* It is in this area that the wisdom of other cultures as well as that of our own can help us attain a greater degree of reconciliation and harmony within the self and in its interpersonal relations.

REFERENCES

Balint, M. (1953), *Primary Love and Psychoanalytic Technique*. New York: Liveright Publishers.

Bowlby, J. (1973), *Attachment and Loss,* Vol. 2, New York: Basic Books.

Burgner, M. and Edgcumbe, R. (1972), Some Problems in Conceptualization of Early Object Relations. Psychoanalytic Study of the Child, 27:283–315.

Fairbairn, R. (1952), *Psychoanalytic Studies of the Personality*. London: Tavistock Publications.

Federn, P. (1952) *Ego Psychology and the Psychoses*. New York: Basic Books.

Freud, A. (1965), *Normality and Pathology in Children*. New York: International Universities Press.

Freud, S. (1938), Splitting of the ego in the process of defense. *Standard Edition,* 23:271–278. London: Hogarth Press, 1962.

Guntrip, H. (1968), *Schizoid Phenomena, Object Relations and the Self*. New York: International Universities Press.

Heinicke, C. & Westheimer, I. (1965), *Brief Separations*. New York: International Universities Press.

Horner, A. (1975), Stages and process in the development of object relations. *Internat. Rev. Psychoanal.* 2(1):95–107.

Kernberg, O. (1976), *Object Relations Theory and Clinical Psychoanalysis*. New York: Jason Aronson.

Khan, M. (1974), *The Privacy of the Self*. New York: International Universities Press.

Klaus, K. & Kennel, J. (1976), *Maternal-Infant Bonding*. St. Louis: Mosby.

Landis, B. (1970), Ego boundaries. In: *Psychological Issues,* Vol. VI, No. 4. New York: International Universities Press.

Levenson, E. (1977), Psychoanalysis—cure or persuasion. This volume, p. 96.

Mahler, M., Pine, F., & Bergman, A. (1975), *The Psychologic Birth of the Infant*. New York: Basic Books.

Nagera, H. (1966), *Early Childhood Disturbances. The Infantile Neurosis and the Adult Disturbance*. New York: International Universities Press.

Nyanaponika, Thera (1973), *The Heart of Buddhist Meditation*. New York: Samuel Weiser.

Piaget, J. (1954), *The Construction of Reality in the Child*. New York: Basic Books.

Pine, F. (1974), Libidinal object constancy. In: *Psychoanalysis and Contemporary Science*. New York: International Universities Press.

Provence, S. & Lipton, R. (1952), *Infants in Institutions: A Comparison of Their Development with Family Reared Infants during the First Year of Life.* New York: International Universities Press.

Sandler, J. & Rosenblatt, B. (1962), The concept of the representational world. The *Psychoanalytic Study of the Child,* 17:128–145. New York: International Universities Press.

Schachtel, E. (1959), *Metamorphosis.* New York: Basic Books, pp. 48–49.

Schecter, D. (1968a), Identification and individuation. *J. Amer. Psychoanal. Assn.,* 16:48–80.

—— (1968b), The oedipus complex: Considerations of ego development and parental interaction. *Contemp. Psychoanal.* 4:111–137.

—— (1973), On the emergence of human relatedness. In: *Interpersonal Explorations in Psychoanalysis: New Directions in Theory and Practice,* ed. E. Witenberg. New York: Basic Books.

—— (1974), Infant development. In: *American Handbook of Psychiatry,* Vol. I, ed. S. Arieti, New York: Basic Books.

—— (1975a), Of human bonds and bondage. *Contemp. Psychoanalysis,* 11:435–452.

—— (1975b), Notes on some basic human developmental tasks. *J. Amer. Acad. Psychoanal.,* 3(3):267–276.

—— & Corman, H. (1971), Some early developments in parent-child interaction. (Unpublished.)

Sendak, M. (1962), *Pierre: A Cautionary Tale.* New York: Harper & Row.

Stern, D. (1971), A micro-analysis of mother-infant interaction: Behavior regulating social contact between a mother and her 3½ month-old twins. *J. Amer. Acad. Child Psychiat.,* 10:501–518.

Sullivan, H. (1953), *The Interpersonal Theory of Psychiatry.* New York: W.W. Norton.

Winnicott, D.W. (1965), *The Maturational Process and the Facilitating Environment.* New York: International Universities Press.

Wolfenstein, M. (1966), How is mourning possible? In: *The Psychoanalytic Study of the Child.* New York: International Universities Press.

7

THE CONSTRUCTIVE POTENTIAL OF IMAGERY AND FANTASY PROCESSES: IMPLICATIONS FOR CHILD DEVELOPMENT, PSYCHOTHERAPY, AND PERSONAL GROWTH

JEROME L. SINGER, Ph.D.

INTRODUCTION: THE RENEWAL OF INTEREST IN FANTASY AND IMAGERY

To ANYBODY but a psychologist it must seem amazing indeed that textbooks on thinking (Bourne, Ekstrand, and Dominowski, 1971; Johnson, 1955) can omit any reference to the stream of consciousness and daydreaming, that introductions to personality (Mischel, 1971) or adolescence (Seidman, 1960) can ignore imagination or fantasy. Yet this has been the case until recently because of psychology's over-emphasis on "public" or observable behavior. Now, after a half-century of repression, imagery is back as a fit subject for formal psychological research (Holt, 1964; Paivio, 1971; Segal, 1971; Sheehan, 1972; J.L. Singer, 1966, 1975a, 1975b). Ongoing thought, the topic proposed for study by William James (1890), remains, however, relatively neglected and primarily the domain of the fine artist.

Indeed, the creative personalities of literature, painting, and cinema were the first to take up James's challenge. The excitement engendered

in the first two decades of this century by the efforts of James Joyce
to produce what Edmund Wilson (1922) has called "perhaps the
most faithful X-ray ever taken of the ordinary human consciousness"
reflected the seriousness with which writers accepted James's insights.
Virginia Woolf wrote in 1919:

> Examine for a moment an ordinary mind on an ordinary day.
> The mind receives a myriad of impressions—trivial, fantastic,
> evanescent, or engraved with the sharpness of steel. From all
> sides they come, an incessant shower of innumerable atoms;
> and as they fall, as they shape themselves into the life of Monday
> or Tuesday the accent falls differently from of old . . . life is not
> a series of gig lamps symmetrically arranged; but a luminous
> halo, a semi-transparent envelope surrounding us from the beginning
> of consciousness to the end. [Woolf, 1953, p. 54].

At the same time that James Joyce, Virginia Woolf and T.S. Eliot
(1919), in his discussion of the "objective correlative," were forming
the basis for the use of the stream of consciousness as a literary and
poetic medium, film makers such as Sergei Eisenstein perceived an opportunity in moving pictures to capture even more effectively the ongoing thought stream. In his development of "montage" and in his
use of "partial representation" to produce images that would evoke in
the viewer the same ongoing thought experience as occurred in the
mind of the artist or of the character represented on the screen, Eisenstein (1942) made another great stride in providing an expression of
ongoing thought.

The effectiveness with which cinema can capture the fleeting but
vivid associations that characterize normal ongoing thought are manifest
in some recent films. In *The Pawnbroker* the tormented protagonist
steps into a New York City subway train and we see a brief flash of a
scene from a cattle car crowded with Jews en route to a concentration
camp—a memory from the pawnbroker's own experience. In *Midnight
Cowboy* the cowboy and his companion, the woeful gamin Ratso Rizzo,
find themselves suddenly at a pseudohippie party. The ever-hungry
Ratso is standing before a buffet table laden with food. He begins
wolfing down sandwiches. Suddenly we see a quick shot of Ratso's
long dead father, a humble shoeshine man wearing his little cap and
standing beside the lavish table. In this poignant second or two of
imagery the director conveys to us Ratso's fantasy: "If only my poor
old dad could be here to enjoy this feast."

The Overemphasis on Verbal and Directed Thought

Not possessing the artist's freedom from the constraints of a scientific method, behavioral scientists have focused much more on the products of specific directed thinking or on the study of isolated features of thought, such as the vividness of images, the effectiveness of imagery in paired-associate learning, and other forms of problem solution. By their very nature the methods of the experimental psychologist have led perhaps to an overweighting of the structured, directed, or "rational" aspects of thought. Studies of concept learning or of abstraction abilities, of various forms of categorical thinking, and of arithmetic or spatial problem solution have predominated because they are easy to set up and control. Only in the most recent years has the individual's ethical thinking been subjected to more careful study or private judgment about human relationships been examined with any degree of systematic effort. Even these researches are generally cast within the format of rational problem solution in a very structured fashion.

The contributions of psychoanalysis, significant as they have been in opening up a broader range of attention to the subtleties of thought and the irrational, wishful, and "selfish" side of private experience, have not fully addressed the nature of ongoing thought. As conscious as Freud was of the many persisting intrusions into adult mental processes of childlike, magical solutions or fantasies, he still tended to assume that the well-analyzed adult would be characterized by much greater use of secondary-process thinking. Indeed, it might be argued that Freud overplayed the logical and formally rational quality of mature waking thought and perhaps underestimated the adaptive and directed quality of wishful, imagery-laden thinking.

Freud's theory of thinking was perhaps the first elaborate effort to develop a comprehensive view of mental process (Rapaport, 1951, 1960). Yet the various structural characteristics of his theory—id, ego, superego; unconscious, preconscious, conscious; primary and secondary processes—were too difficult to fit together because they were developed at different times and were never brought into correspondnce (Gill, 1963).

Some attempted modification of this excessively rational view of mature thought processes was introduced by such psychoanalysts as Ernst Kris (1951), who proposed that at least with creative thought one should look for "regression in the service of the ego." Again, the term "regression" seems to continue the earlier emphasis on the directed, rational, "secondary process" quality of mature adult thought. To assert that the poet who can recapture early childhood memories or fantasies, but can also make unusual and odd combinations from current experiences, is relying on a more childlike mode of thought seems unsatisfactory. This approach seems, for one thing, to place excessive emphasis on verbal or language processes as being of a higher order than auditory or visual imagery content in adult thinking. Probably this prejudice is pervasive among professionals largely because they depend so much on the ultimate verbal expression of material in print. It seems unlikely that the brain of a Beethoven or a Bach, teeming with melody, with novel and original combinations of themes, instrumental coloration and interweaving lines of music, should be viewed as representing a somehow more primitive style of thought than that of a mathematician solving algebra problems. The recent heightened awareness of the differential processing capacities of the brain and its functional asymmetry for verbal-quantitative and imagery-spatial representational capacities suggests that the process of effective thought is far more complex than has been recognized. In addition, if we free ourselves of the hydraulic energy models that characterized so much of the theory about thinking for the first 60 years of the century and substitute information-processing models, then we can free ourselves of the oversymplified primary-secondary process or regression views that have been a part of that model.

A basic problem in our understanding of ongoing human thought, has to do with the fact that we inevitably rely on some aspect of language to determine the nature of private experience. This often makes the report on thinking very much subject to the demands of the given task. Most people who have written about thought in the past have tended to value logic and analytic capacities and have attempted to express their ideas via the most formal aspects of communication. This mode of expression has led them almost inevitably to brush aside or to ignore the many intrusions of visual or auditory or other images into their thinking in the interests of providing a refined product. Similarly, by the setting of tasks, such as the formation of concepts, often using abstract geometric forms themselves alien to most people's day-to-day experience, these writers have seriously underestimated the degree to which most thinking has to do with interpersonal situations and human relationships. Indeed, one may even assert that Piaget, who has done so much to develop a cognitive or information-processing alternative to the drive model of thinking, has also tended to a great extent to neglect the degree to which ongoing thought has reference to social interactions rather than simply to the characteristics of the physical world. Questionnaire responses from hundreds of subjects have indicated that most people devote a good deal of time to speculation in daydreams about human relationships and the patterns of social interaction around them (J.L. Singer, 1975a, 1975b). Again it is only very recently that psychologists have addressed themselves more systematically to the important cognitive implications of thinking about people, their faces, their intentions, and the ethics of social situations (Izard, 1977; Kohlberg, 1966; Rosenthal, 1914; Selman, 1975; Tomkins, 1962–1963). A pet peeve of mine is the habit of psychoanalysts who persist in using the term "object representations" when talking about the way human beings are characterized in ongoing everyday thought and daydreams.

HEMISPHERIC ASYMMETRY AND THE DUAL CODING SYSTEM

Recent discoveries in brain research as well as in studies of information processing suggest a framework for integrating the phenomenological evidence of the importance of our imagery capacities and of ongoing thought processes within an adaptive model of mature normal functioning. Although the critical role of the brain's left hemisphere for receptive and expressive language function has long been known, the functions of the right hemisphere were not well understood until reports on "split brain" patients began to appear (Bogen, 1969; Gazzaniga, 1967; Sperry, 1968). Subsequently, studies of perception, imagery, reflective thought, affective expression and personality differences have increasingly converged to clarify some of the special properties of the right hemisphere of the brain (Bakan, 1969, 1971; Kinsbourne, 1971, 1973; Kocel et al., 1972; Morgan, McDonald, and McDonald, 1971; Rodin and Singer, 1977; Rosenberg, 1977; Schwartz, Davidson and Maer, 1975). These studies suggest that right-hemisphere functions include visual and auditory imagery, spatial representation, pure melodic thought, fantasy, and the emotional components of ongoing thought.

Quite independently a sizable body of research on cognitive processes has generated evidence that our thinking and information-storage and retrieval processes necessitate the postulation of at least two major coding systems, a *verbal* or *linguistic* system that functions sequentially;

for instance, a sentence takes time to be presented; and an *imagery* or *spatial* representational system that operates by parallel processing; for example, we imagine the face of a friend in one instantaneous configuration (Paivio, 1971; J.L. Singer, 1974). The verbal coding system with its abstract, analytic properties is especially efficient for integrating tremendously diverse phenomena into one language label or formula that allows extremely rapid retrieval later on. Consider all the very different-looking objects that satisfy the label "chair" or the tremendous range of phenomena summarized in the formula $E=mc^2$. The more global, concrete quality of the imagery system has the special value of providing detail when no verbal label has been stored, as in an artist's sketches of different possibilities for the face of a criminal or in descriptions of the interior of a room. Research suggests that concrete imagery is helpful in paired-associate learning (Paivio, 1971), especially when recognition as opposed to instant retrieval is what is called for, because the brain can store a fantastic number of specific faces or objects with only one reasonably long exposure.

The dual coding system has distinct advantages for normal adaptation. Research by Seamon (1972), for example, suggests that learning is best when one encodes not only the verbal label of an event, but a concrete image as well. Poets and fine writers long ago learned that they communicate best when they express their thoughts through metaphors, analogies, and other concrete images. Keats's closing lines to "Ode on a Grecian Urn"—"Beauty is truth, truth beauty"—might leave us cold or puzzled had he not preceded this abstraction by vivid images and fantasies about the figures depicted on the amphora.

Viewed from the perspective of a dual coding system as an essential feature of human information processing, imagery and daydreams or fantasy need not be regarded as "regressive" phenomena or manifestations of a primary or immature process as psychoanalytic lore suggests. Schachtel (1959) has suggested that the socialization of the individual often involves increased reliance on "empty" verbal clichés or abstractions with a loss of the direct contact with experience implicit in the concrete modality–specific imagery system. We respond to great writers often because they reawaken in us the possibilities of direct experience through their detailed reconstruction of specific sights, sounds, or smells. Careful counts of images have demonstrated that Shakespeare excelled his contemporaries not only in the number of specific images he employed in his plays and poems, but also in the range of sensory modalities involved. Where Marlowe's imagery was largely visually oriented, Shakespeare refers to smell, touch, and taste in concrete ways again and again as well as to sight and sound. Recall the reference to Falstaff as an "old tub of guts" or Hamlet's comment to the Danish courtiers seeking to locate the hidden body of poor murdered Polonius, ". . . if you find him not within this month, you shall nose him as you go up the stairs into the lobby."

The advantages of the concrete properties of imagery associated with right-brain function for psychotherapy are manifold. Of special importance, as we shall see in specific examples cited later, is the fact that imagery creats a context, a vivid immediacy of experience that allows the fuller expression of emotion, the re-creation of related but often unlabeled memories. In effect, context permits the emergence of what has been called the repressed but what may actually be better viewed as unretrievable experience because no distinct verbal encoding has occurred with the original event. Without the advantage of a concise verbal label a memory cannot be reinstated without re-establishing a appropriate context through visual or auditory or other imagery. Recall Proust's description of the flooding back of memories of his childhood at Combray when by chance in adult life he tastes a madeleine soaked in tea.

Sullivan (1956), with his notion of the prototaxic mode, anticipated the significance of verbal labeling for retrieval. Children who experience frightening events at an age before they acquire an adequate vocabulary that helps them place events in context and label them at the same time, may grow up with a stored set of visual or auditory experiences that continue to influence other related experiences without being identified in themselves, unless, in effect, an environmental situation is established that re-creates circumstances comparable to this early stored memory material. We realize today that individuals can store tremendous amounts of material visually without verbal labels (Shepherd, 1967). They simply cannot retrieve the material effectively unless they are shown pictures of the material and are required to indicate whether or not they have ever seen such things before. This method of recognition in experimental psychology has been used, for example, in research with nonliterate groups to indicate that a glance through something equivalent to a Sears Roebuck catalog where as many as 500 objects can be seen, that are not identifiable by any verbal label in the language of the particular culture, can still be recognized months afterward and discriminated clearly from a whole set of other objects that were not previously seen at all.

In effect, many forms of psychotherapy attempt to establish conditions that will re-create circumstances allowing the stored images to be evoked. In the past a variety of reasons have been given for the use of such methods, including an almost mythical belief in birth experiences, as in such techniques as the primal scream. It is likely that many of these approaches in effect maximize the likelihood that unlabeled but stored visual or auditory images will be retrieved. Even in classical psychoanalysis the use of the couch, where one adult reclines in the presence of another adult who is seated, re-creates a psychological situation that has similarities to early childhood behavior for example, when the child is put to bed and perhaps even told a story by an adult seated nearby. The very nature of the social situation established in a classical psychoanalysis brings about a context, supported by emphasis on imagery components such as the recall of dreams or fantasies, that enhances the likelihood of the patient's re-creating childlike memories and attitudes. This phenomenon is reflected in the occurrence of transference (J.L. Singer, 1974).

It is remarkable how effectively re-creating or directly re-experiencing contexts related to earlier significant life experiences can restore a series of images and also associated affective responses in keeping with the setting. During the grueling 1976 presidential campaign both President Ford and his challenger, Jimmy Carter, showed remarkable self-control in a variety of difficult settings and circumstances, including the awkward 20 minutes of silence occasioned by equipment failure in their first televised debate before 50 or 60 million Americans. Both men finally "broke down" in tears on returning to their home towns, in settings where they were surrounded by old friends and family figures. Indeed, Carter's weeping was in the context of greeting old friends in Plains, Georgia as his mother stood beside him on the day after his election.

Horowitz (1970) has proposed that we view stored behavior along three dimensions, a verbal-lexical dimension, an imagery dimension, and a motor-enactive dimension. Presumably each of these dimensions has different general areas of brain control or representation with the verbal system largely coordinated through the left hemisphere of the brain, the imagery system through the right hemisphere of the brain, and the motor-enactive system, the action component of our behavior, through the cortical motor areas and the limbic system. Whereas most behavior involves complex combinations of these systems, there are important differences between them in implication, as we have suggested. As we shall see below, it is possible to conceive of various goals and techniques of specific types of psychotherapy as emphasizing one or another of these three systems. (Table I.)

The important point to be made here is that instead of viewing imagery as an early developmental form that must be superseded by the verbal-lexical system, it is important to recognize that both imagery and verbal systems continue throughout adult life to be equally important.[1] Without the capacity to use imagery to explore the future and the past, we may not be able to re-establish adequate contexts to retrieve many kinds of early childhood memories that have important implications. In addition, the concreteness of imagery permits the reinvoking of strong emotional response, something most therapists recognize as critical in helping patients to recognize the complexity of their experiences and to encourage them to seek to change their behavior and ways of looking at the world.

Some controversy still exists as to whether the imagery and emotional components of behavior are both located in the right hemisphere, or whether the evocation of imagery itself simply increases the likelihood of a strong emotional reaction. One can see how the vividness of a concrete image can generate emotion in contrast with an abstract statement. In therapy patients often will say such things as, "I guess I had a typical oedipal family—a doting mother and a strong father who made me feel very inadequate." Such a statement is not very useful, as most therapists recognize, unless the patient actually produces a specific memory or scene describing in vivid detail an interaction between the child and parents or cites a movie or play that evokes similar experiences.

A simple thought experiment I have used to demonstrate how emotion is closely linked to the evocation of vivid specific modality-related imagery is the following. Take the following abstract assertion: "The consequences of our actions evoked the wrath of the authorities." If, instead of this abstract phrase, we substitute the metaphor: "That's when the shit hit the fan!" and try further to image vividly through each sense—smell, sight, sound, touch, and taste—the consequences of "shit hitting a fan," we can reinvoke the emotional experience of bringing down upon oneself the wrath of the authorities!

---

[1] In his *The Origin of Consciousness in the Breakdown of the Bicameral Mind* Julian Jaynes (1977) suggests a sweeping and imaginative hypothesis— that the development of the human sense of private experience and personal thought occurred relatively late in evolution (c. 1400 B.C.), when the right half of the brain was no longer the source of the "hallucinatory voices" believed by people to be direct communications from the gods.

Table 1

Technical variations in the psychotherapeutic uses of imagery

Encoding Systems		Direction of System Shift or "Technique"
1. Verbal-sequential (Horowitz's *lexical*) (left-hemisphere function)		
2. Motor-kinesthetic (Horowitz's *enactive*) (limbic-motor areas, etc.)		
3. Imagery (visual, auditory, spatial) — parallel (Horowitz's image)[b] (right-hemisphere function)		

Therapeutic Orientation	Objective or Symptom Focus	Direction of System Shift or "Technique"
1. Hypnosis	Symptom - relief or improved recall	Intense concentration on each encoding system individually. Motor → verbal → imagery
2. Psychoanalysis	Insight and ego expansion	Imagery → verbal-sequential
a. Dream interpretation	a. Overcome resistance — enhance affect ideational integrative	Imagery → verbal-sequential → joint verbal-imagery integration
b. Transference analysis	b. Identify unlabeled childhood parental memories and fantasies	
	c. Sharpen interpersonal discrimination from treatment to daily life	
3. Raich's character analysis; Perls's Gestalt therapy	Freeing and redirecting energy	Motor-kinesthetic → imagery → motor
4. European "mental imagery" approaches (Desoille's guided daydream)	Resymbolization symptom relief	Verbal-sequential → imagery or imagery (1) → imagery (2)

Table 1 *(continued)*

5. Gendlin's focusing (Rogerian)	Expanded self-awareness	Verbal or motor → imagery affective
6. Kelly's personal construct therapy	Improved role discrimination and role enactment	Verbal → imagery → verbal → motor
7. Wolpe's systematic desensitization	Relief of phobic symptoms	Motor → imagery → motor
8. Covert aversive conditioning (behavior modification)	Symptom relief, control of compulsions, unwanted thoughts, or behaviors	Imagery → Motor → imagery (1) kinesthetic (2)
9. Bandura's symbolic mediation	Symptom relief and self-regulation	(Perception) → imagery → motor
10. Ellis's rational-emotive or cognitive theories	Sympton, relief, self-regulation, self-assertiveness	Verbal → imagery-affect → verbal (1) (2)

[b] Imagery system ordinarily more closely tied to affect expression and experience.

IMAGERY AND MAKE-BELIEVE IN CHILDHOOD

Whereas in the past imagery has been viewed as a characteristic of the child that gradually fades in later life, other evidence (Rohwer, 1970) suggests that the elaborative skills needed for effective vocabulary development in childhood hinge on imagery development. The attempts at transformation range from simple use of the plastic spoon to feed a doll (Fein, 1975) to the more elaborate make-believe of the four-or five-year-old where blocks become fortresses or pipe cleaners become heroes and heroines. These and other more complicated transformations seem to some extent to require the child's interpolation of a visual or auditory private image. Indeed the indications are that as children grow somewhat older and create more complex forms of make-believe, they prefer less well defined objects and choose instead more unstructured playthings because these lend themselves to more varied private transformation and do not come into conflict with the private "images of the child" (Fein and Robertson, 1974; Pulaski, 1973).

The child who plays at make-believe may be attempting to construct sights and sounds, smells, touches, and tastes as part of pretending games and in this sense may actually be practicing and sharpening his capacity for the use of imagery. Our imagery capacities, in addition to helping us remember things, also heighten esthetic experience and human sensitivity (Schachtel, 1959). Imagery skills assist us in appreciating the beauties of nature and, in restrospect, they help us relive a fine piece of music or a lovely sunset. Such a sensuous approach to a fine painting may help us appreciate what Bernson has called the tactile values of the Renaissance masters. The delight one takes in the first view of the sunlit hills of Tuscany may actually be enhanced by the fact that we have already seen them in our memories of the paintings by Giotto or Fra Filippo Lippi.

Imaginative Play and Verbal Fluency or Divergent Thinking

We have already indicated the extent to which imagery and verbal skills may interact as part of the child's early pretending activity. An obvious feature of pretending games is that the child in his uninhibited way speaks out loud many of his thoughts in what Piaget (1932) has called egocentric speech. Piaget describes how two children engage in play alongside each other. Each one describes his own behavior and rarely actually communicates despite the appearance of a conversation.

One of the characteristics of talking out loud for the child is that the child to some extent hears his own vocalization. In other words, even in the absence of adults talking directly with the child, which we know enhances verbal skills, the child's own verbalizations during make-believe provide an ongoing source of verbal stimulation. The sound effects or scraps of dialogue the child emits in the course of a pretend game create a stimulus field to which the child may make further response or from which he may acquire further information in the same way that our own ongoing thoughts provide an alternative stimulus field.

More extended discussions of possible relations between the enrichment of vocabulary, labeling capacities, and the development of capacity for divergent thinking or what is sometimes called creative expression in the verbal area have been presented in J.L. Singer (1973) and Smilansky (1968). Generally speaking, the position one can take is that the child engaging in make-believe play not only practices words already learned and tries to fit them into his limited range of cognitive schema (a part of the accommodation-assimilation cycle of Piaget), but because of the very limited range of these schema, the child in effect creates some novelty to which he makes a further response. The quaintness or cuteness of the child's behavior from the adult standpoint lie in the inappropriate linkage of words to make-believe play. A child of my acquaintance was seen lining up a host of plastic cowboys and soldiers in full battle array. When asked what this was about by his mother, he replied he was getting them ready to rescue his father because he had heard his mother say that Daddy would not be home for dinner because "Daddy is all tied up at work."

The various outlandish possibilities provided by the child's attempts at accommodation and assimilation to a still very limited differentated schema system probably provoke the positive affects of surprise and interest in the controlled atmosphere of a play situation. These positive emotions may explain why make-believe play in general shows longer sequences and complex combinatorial possibilities. The child seeks out situations of moderate levels of increasing stimulation and when reducing such moderate levels also experiences joy in accordance with the theoretical propositions of Tomkins (1962–1963), as elaborated in J.L. Singer (1973). We would therefore expect that the child would not only make progress in the convergent processes of actually refining word definitions by the feedback coming from ongoing make-believe, but would also become aware of odd and divergent possibilities in the use of vocabulary from his initial makeshift efforts at including snatches of adult conversation or gesture into the ongoing plot of a pretend game.

Marshall and Hahn (1967) have found some indications that middle-class children trained in sociodramatic play subsequently did increase the level of spontaneous role playing and related activities in the course of their play. There were also indications of increased associative fluency in the children. Smilansky (1968) has carried out a very extensive experiment making use of imaginative play training exercises with both middle and lower socioeconomic group Israeli children. Her intention here was to help the children move more smoothly into the school situation. In her analysis of the data, Smilansky found that the increased fantasy play training of the experimental group led subsequently to an increase in verbal communication between children who had been relatively inarticulate earlier and also to the use of more parts of speech in verbalization.

Two studies (Feitelson, 1972; Feitelson and Ross, 1973) both examine the effects of training on increasing the complexity of play in children and also the level of creativity as measured by instruments such as those developed by Torrance (1966). These studies, generally carried out with children from lower socioeconomic backgrounds, attempted to control for amount of interaction between child and adult and for other important independent variables. The data indicate that the play training itself did considerably increase the complexity of the spontaneous play behavior of the children; there were also indications of increased verbal fluency and particularly originality of verbal communication in the children. The overall impact of the series of studies carried out by Feitelson suggests that novel and original ways of looking at material as well as more sophisticated combinatorial behaviors are an outgrowth of opportunities to model or otherwise observe make-believe play.

If one looks at the issue of divergent production as a basic part of overall intellectual growth in the same way that simple vocabulary skills represent the convergent processes that are necessary (Kagan and Kogan, 1970; J.L. Singer, 1973; Wallach, 1971), then the relation of imaginative play to creative or divergent productions does emerge, particularly with older children. The work of Saltz and Johnson (1973) indicates that systematic training of children in an urban ghetto area effectively enhanced their ability to produce more thoroughly rounded thematic stories and in general evinced stimulation of storytelling capacities. A study by Litt (1973) has yielded evidence that children who reported more imaginative play as part of their day-to-day activities at the ten-year-old level and up were more likely to score higher on measures of divergent thinking. These measures, of course, depend heavily on effective vocabulary expression.

A study by Gottlieb (1973) indicates that modeling effects of a teacher who produced imaginative material increased the likelihood that junior high school children would tell more complex and imaginative stories to an abstract film. A somewhat older age group was less susceptible to the influence of the model and more likely to respond in terms of their prior predisposition to imagination (as measured by their Rorschach human movement response).

Pulaski (1973) has found that five- and six-year-old children predisposed to make-believe play (based on Rorschach scores and an interview about their own home play activities) were much more inclined to play imaginatively with unstructured blocks and could, in addition, introduce a shift in point of view when presented with the task of playing with an object in a different way than they had been required to play with it on a previous day. That is, having initially played with a cowboy as a cowboy, they were asked subsequently to play with him as a flyer or a pilot; the more imaginatively predisposed children could move relatively easily into this transformation.

The trend does seem to suggest that opportunities for make-believe play, whether engaged in spontaneously by the child as part of an ongoing predisposition or whether fostered by some more formal modeling or specific training procedures, do lead to an enhancement both of the effective use of ordinary vocabulary skills and also of an ability to develop even more complicated narrative lines in either the play itself or the production of thematic responses to material presented by adults. It certainly appears that we are here on the threshold of some rather important possibilities that have implications for education (J.L. Singer, 1977). Parents can stimulate better language and school readiness in their children through encouraging imaginative play (D.G. Singer and J.L. Singer, 1977). Teachers should be able to help kindergarteners and early school age children play at make-believe games as part of helping them develop excitement about reading and also help them develop imaginative skills.

Imagination and Reality

Elsewhere I have suggested on the basis of primarily clinical observation and theoretical speculation that the experience of engaging in make-believe play may actually help the child discriminate fantasy from reality more effectively (J.L. Singer, 1966, 1973). My reasoning is based in part on the notion that the child's ability to produce transformations also offers the child experience in recognizing those sequences produced by himself and those demanded by others or the characteristics of the physical environment. A consequence of active play and replay of make-believe sequences may also be an enhancement of differentiated memory schema. Using reasoning of this kind, Tucker (1975) has shown that subjects with a high fantasy predisposition (as measured by human movement responses on Rorschach-type inkblots) recall an adventure story more completely and accurately, with more embellishments, than do subjects with very little fantasy predisposition. This result occurred irrespective of whether the material was presented as fictional or as true. Tucker also proposes that high fantasy predisposition leads to more effective recall of fictional stories than of stories described as true. Finally, she advances some hypotheses about differential functional set and the duration of time after full recall.

Her subjects were 134 children with relatively normal IQs falling within the range of 90–125. The children were mostly 11 years old with a range from 9 to 12. There were two conditions of recall, immediate and long-term, and two conditions of story presentation, fictional or true. The latter conditions were reversed for control purposes, thus producing eight experimental conditions.

As stated above, the high-fantasy children showed superior performance on completeness of story response, on accuracy of story response, and on embellishment of the story. However, there was no correlation between the fantasy predisposition and the long-term recall condition or the story's presumed truth or falsity. A more detailed analysis of the specific kinds of errors made by subjects in recall indicated that the high-fantasy subjects showed significantly less likelihood of disruptive errors, that is, breaks in continuity, serious distortion, or introduction of new and inaccurate information. This contrasted with relatively small differences between the groups in simple mistakes, such as differences in the total number of people engaging in the search for the lost children (one of the incidents used in the experiment).

Tucker also measured fantasy predisposition by including at the end of the experiment a questionnaire based on the work of J.L. Singer (1961, 1973) which inquired about the spontaneous imaginative-play characteristics of the children. Children more prone to engaging in make-believe games or to reporting an imaginary companion were more likely to have shown higher levels of accuracy in recall of the units of the scores, to have made fewer mistakes, and, particularly, to have made fewer disruptive errors. It should be noted, incidentally, that the measures of fantasy did not correlate significantly with intelligence.

This study is perhaps the first to have approached the question so often raised about the possible risks of imaginative play. The group of 11-year-olds who are predisposed to make-believe turn out to be more accurate in recall of story material and less prone to introduce gross distortion in it than children who lack comparable imaginative predisposition. This approach of examining recall in the context of emotionally laden material would appear to open the way for a new avenue of exploration and seems closer to issues raised clinically about the value or danger of fantasy behavior in childhood.

Imaginative Play and Self-Entertainment or Waiting Behavior

I have proposed elsewhere (J.L. Singer, 1961, 1966, 1973) that a significant advantage of the capacity of children to engage in imaginative games or for adults to engage in waking fantasy or daydreaming lies in the likelihood that such behavior creates a novel stimulus field. This may be viewed in some circumstances as an escape from an unpleasant environment, but one may also see it as a means for coping with a situation in which there is considerable redundancy. Such is often the case in routine bus trips to work or, for a child, the seemingly endless wait before a medical examination or while mother is having her hair done. The danger in such waiting situations lies in the fact that without some form of self-entertainment, the time seems to drag endlessly. Extensive research indicates that "filled time" appears to pass much more rapidly than unfilled time.

For the child the situation is more difficult because at relatively early ages reading is not available to "fill time." The child becomes restless and, even if some of his physical exploration of the room may be a manifestation of a competent searching activity, he may very quickly provoke the wrath of parents or other authority figures by perhaps tipping over an ashtray or bumping against the lamp. For the child who has no private resources and cannot generate an ongoing make-believe game even with relatively unstructured playthings, the likelihood of coming into conflict with adults in the many inevitable waiting situations of this type is great. Indeed, clinical indications are that children who have difficulty in concentration along this line often are subject to considerable negative affective reaction from adults. After a while such active children are labeled as "bad," "wild," or "pesky." A waiting experience under such circumstances can degenerate into a combination of screaming and whining and even lead to blows.

Research with adults suggests that individuals engaged in positive fantasy activity are less likely to experience time as having dragged (Wheeler, 1969). In addition, there is evidence that individuals already showing indications of imaginativeness, based on Rorschach scores of human movement (Singer, 1960), are likely to be able to tolerate waiting-room situations with a minimum of restlessness; mental patients are also less likely to be impulsive or prone to aggressive behavior in their ward routines (J.L. Singer and Opler, 1956; J.L. Singer, Wilsensky, and McCraven, 1956).

In the case of children the evidence is also available, although not as extensive. Riess (1957) found that children at kindergarten age who had numerous human movement responses in response to the Barron inkblots were more likely to remain quietly occupied during an extended waiting period. Spivack and Levine (1964), studying adolescents, also report that those subjects who showed more evidence of imaginative behavior as measured by inkblots and other indices were more likely to avoid serious disciplinary problems; the children low in imaginative tendencies showed difficulties in self-regulation and were more often involved in acts of delinquency and other antisocial behaviors.

Elsewhere I have reported a study specifically addressed to the question of the waiting behavior of children and its association with their ongoing play behavior (J.L. Singer, 1961). Children between ages six and nine were given an opportunity to simulate astronauts by sitting quietly in an imaginary capsule for as long as they possibly could. Results indicated that those children who reported more make-believe play as part of their ongoing repertory of activities and also reported more imaginary companions were more likely to be able to tolerate the long wait and to hold out during the simulated capsule situation. Observations of the children's pattern of dealing with the enforced delay indicated that the children who had reported more make-believe to start with sustained themselves during the waiting period by introducing play elements into the situation—mouthing sound effects and occasionally gesturing as if they were actually participating in a space flight.

Again, results from this study and a subsequent one carried out with three- and four-year-olds (Singer, 1973) have generally supported the notion that imaginative play behavior is likely to be associated with somewhat greater abilities in concentration and on the creation of a positive affective atmosphere. Recent studies by Mischel, Zeiss, and

Zeiss (1974) have indicated that where children anticipate positively reinforcing experiences to be produced by their own activities rather than provided from outside, waiting behavior or delay of gratification is more prolonged. In a study by Franklin (1975) expectations of positive reinforcement in preschoolers were positively correlated with imaginative play predisposition and with duration of spontaneous imaginative play. Expectation of negative reinforcement was negatively correlated with imaginative play.

Nahme-Huang, et al. (1977), studying an older group of hospitalized emotionally disturbed children, also found a significant positive correlation between expectation of positive internal reinforcement and imaginative play predisposition as measured by interview and inkblot scores. In general, children expecting more positive internal reinforcements tended to show more imaginative play, more positive emotionality during free play, and less overt aggression.

The work of Mischel and collaborators (Mischel, 1973) has indicated that when children engage in some form of consistent self-communication, they are able to maintain a longer period of delay of gratification or to defer overt responsiveness more effectively. The research of Meichenbaum (1975) and various collaborators has also pointed up the possibility that children who engage in self-communications and practice a variety of imagery-related cognitive procedures can learn to control impulsivity more effectively.

Imaginative Play and Affect

Surprisingly little attention has been paid to the child's ongoing emotional life as expressed during spontaneous play behavior. One of the major characteristics observed in imaginative play is the rise and fall of excitement and the liveliness and joy that children exhibit as part of the game. Make-believe play is closely related to Piaget's accommodation-assimilation cycle in the young child. This cycle, however, is not a purely cognitive one. It involves as much an alternation of affective reactions aroused by the differential rate of complex material that has to be assimilated by the child. This general theoretical position reflects an extension of Tomkins's (1962–1963) theory which gives affect, rather than drive, the central role in human motivation and which also definitively points to the close relation between affective behavior and the rate and persistence of new cognitive inputs with which the organism is dealing. If we assume the child is confronted with a great deal of novelty, which might arouse the affects of surprise or interest, this could account for some of the continuous replaying of complex material until it can eventually be assimilated into established schema and a match made with previously learned material. It is this match that produces the smiling response or other overt manifestations of joy and elation.

The earliest origins of make-believe play seem to center around the child's attempt to reproduce actions observed in adults, such as feeding or other caretaking responses. Again, one frequently sees the child's puzzled look as he attempts to control and manipulate a spoon or pick up a toy telephone. Then, as the motor skill is acquired to manipulate the object or words of an adult are repeated ("yummy-yum-yummy-yummy!" or "hello-hello!" on the telephone), there is often a peal of laughter or a broad grin. This pattern is further enhanced by the very nature of the interaction that goes on between adults and children and that also undoubtedly plays a role in the development of imaginative play. The early games of "peek-a-boo" initiated by parents with children often involve a combination of mild mystery for the child followed by recognition of a familiar object. With very young children in the initiation of this game, the novel material is often presented at a rate just a bit too rapid for the child and one sees the facial expression of puzzlement and almost perhaps a bit of fear. As Tomkins (1962–1963) and Izard (1971) have pointed out, material that is presented at too rapid a rate for organization will evoke the affect of fear or even terror. For the child the first disappearance of an object is frightening indeed, but very quickly he is reassured by its reappearance and the smiling face of the parent. Once the whole pattern in which new material can be viewed under some control appears, then it can be dealt with in the form of a game. Soon it becomes assimilated to established schema and evokes the affect of joy. Joy or the smiling response in this system are occasioned by the reduction of a high level of complexity to an established schema.

Much parent-child interaction involves this kind of subtle mixture of both cognitive and affective interactions. It should be stressed that the facial expression of the parent and the amount of information communicated by the face is perhaps a critical part of the whole affective response (Eckman, Friessen, and Ellsworth, 1971; Izard, 1971; Tomkins, 1962–1963). The parent's smile is perhaps the single most reinforcing experience the child has apart from satisfaction of the basic body needs of hunger, thirst, or relief of pain.

Sutton-Smith (1975) has called attention to the extent to which imaginative play seems to provide some degree of power for the child over situations that are ordinarily too difficult for him to grasp, either intellectually or physically. Make-believe, by giving the child a control of pacing, enhances a sense of power and thus evokes a generally positive affective response pattern.

In summary, then, there is a growing body of evidence that imaginative play in early childhood is an important constructive feature of normal development. Psychotherapists have for many years, of course, relied on spontaneous play as a treatment method for disturbed children. It is increasingly being recognized that training teachers or parents to assist children from an early age to develop their imaginative skills may have preventive implications in the area of mental health (J.L. Singer and D.G. Singer, 1976; J.L. Singer, 1977). Specific approaches to helping children increase the level of spontaneous make-believe have been developed and tested and are relatively easy to institute with pliable preschoolers or 5-year-olds (Freyberg, 1973; Saltz, Dixon and Johnson, 1976; D.G. Singer and J.L. Singer, 1977; Smilansky, 1968). The literature also suggests that imaginative capacities in children may make them less susceptible to the more dangerous, violence-imitative aspects of television (Biblow, 1973). Imaginative play and positive emotions of joy and liveliness are closely associated in a variety of researches (J.L. Singer and D.C. Singer, 1976). A recent study under the direction of Dorothy Singer and myself (as yet unpublished) indicates that nursery school children who play imaginatively are not only more likely to smile and show less anger or sadness, but they are also more cooperative and constructive in interaction with others. Training in imaginative play has also been at least temporarily effective in work with severely emotionally disturbed children in a state hospital (Nahme-Huang, et al., 1977). The prospects of an emphasis of fostering make-believe play and imaginative games seem promising indeed.

IMAGERY AND GUIDED DAYDREAM APPROACHES TO PSYCHOTHERAPY

Systematic attention to people's imagery capacity has characterized a range of recent developments in psychotherapy. An extensive examination of the ways in which imagery has been employed in classical and neo-Freudian psychoanalysis; in the newer European guided daydream psychotherapies, such as Desoille's (1961) *Le Rêve Eveillé Dirigé;* and increasingly in the panoply of behavior-modification techniques, has been presented elsewhere (J.L. Singer, 1974). The various uses of imagery seem in many ways to provide a basis for linking the seemingly diverse approaches that characterize modern psychotherapy. Indeed, it is possible that a systematic analysis of the different ways in which the verbal capacities and imagery resources of the human cognitive system are employed may provide us with a common basis for understanding what various psychotherapies have in common with respect not only to technique, but also to objective. Table 1, which combines suggestions by Horowitz (1970, 1975) and myself (J.L. Singer, 1974), represents an application of the distinction made at the outset of this chapter between the verbal and imagery encoding systems to the apparent objectives and methods of various psychotherapies.

Although this table is sure to offend representatives from the various schools who may feel that their approaches represent more complex aims and methods, it does seem likely that some valid differences exist between the psychotherapies highlighted here. For example, the classical psychoanalytic method aims at a comprehensive reorganization of the total personality. It seems to rely, to a great extent, on assisting the patient to translate many forms of interior monologue and verbal free association into the more concrete manifestations of imagery. Then it attempts to provide more differentiated and adequate labeling systems for such concrete experiences as will enhance the subsequent effective use of both verbal and imagery methods in normal thought and cognitive appraisal.

By contrast, many of the European mental imagery methods emphasize the translation of verbal experience into imagery as the core of the method and do not attempt in any systematic way to reformulate imagery experiences in terms of verbal labels or linguistic shorthand. In effect, a change is sought in the undercurrent of ongoing symbolic representations that are part of human experience, with the belief that such changes will lead to efficacious modifications, not only in experience, but in behavior or interpersonal relationships. A minimum of emphasis is placed, therefore, on verbal encoding and verbal formulation of the "imagery trips" that characterize this procedure.

The Gestalt therapy approach, at least as formulated in action by Perls (1970) in his weekend demonstration groups, attempts to translate body postures, which may in a sense be called frozen forms of kinesthetic memory, back into an imagery modality, often with associated memories from early childhood as well as from recent experience. The systematic retranslation of such images into a verbal encoding system is often minimized, however, because the goal of the treatment is formulated in terms of enhancing direct experience rather than intellectual understanding or linguistic encoding.

In this chapter I have tried to focus primarily on specific practical uses of imagery available to the psychotherapist and, by extension, ultimately useful in daily life, perhaps as a form of self-development or prevention of disurbance. These approaches, drawn from a variety of psychotherapies, are not intended to be comprehensive, but rather suggestive of how far one can indeed go through systematic analysis of the imagery capacities we all seem to possess.

Imagery Usage in Psychoanalysis and Related Psychodynamic Approaches

I have elsewhere discussed at length the origin of Freud's use of an imagery association method out of his early employment of hypnosis (J.L. Singer, 1974). Indeed, Freud (1962) in the period before the appearance of *The Interpretation of Dreams* in 1900 placed considerably greater emphasis on an imagery association system, held the patient's head, and encouraged a stream of visual pictures. This approach later shifted toward the rule of verbal free association, and it can be argued that Freud may have lost some of the power of the method in his allowing the patient the freedom of a more verbal associative pattern (Reyher, 1963; J.L. Singer, 1974). It is possible that Freud was somewhat suspicious of pure imagery and, with his own great emphasis on rationality, tended to view the visual or purely auditory imagery that characterized dreams and fantasies as regressive phenomena that needed ultimately to be translated into verbal formulations. It was clear to Freud that one could only reach the unconscious through concrete manifestations of imagery as represented in dreams or in the analysis of transference fantasies. He may, however, have seriously underestimated the adaptive power of man's imagery capacity, and this error may have led to the relative slowness and often considerable redundancy that characterizes the modern psychoanalytic method as a clinical intervention procedure.

Individual psychotherapists and psychoanalysts have always relied on the patient's capacity to produce imagery to circumvent obvious defensiveness or resistance. Ferenczi (1950) was extremely sensitive in his clinical work to inhibitions of motor activity, which he was able to show could often, when translated into imagery, yield important insights about longstanding fantasies or irrational fears of particular patients. Indeed, he would have a patient who showed a mannerism, such as foot swinging while seated, inhibit that movement. He then found that an image occurred to the patient, often revealing important recurring fantasies. This translation of motor activity into imagery was also adopted by Reich (1945) and has become a feature of the Gestalt approach to psychotherapy.

A simple example from my own clinical experience may indicate how a shift from a verbal pattern to an imagery system may turn out to be extremely useful in opening the way for greater understanding by the patient, as well as being an indication within the therapeutic session. A patient of mine, a woman in her early fifties, began a session with recurrent comments that she could think of nothing to say, that nothing seemed to be coming to her mind, and that she was simply feeling uncomfortable because there seemed to be no way of getting started. I encouraged her to lean back for a moment, shut her eyes, and allow whatever image occurred to develop as fully as possible, and then to report it to me. She complied with my request, and then produced the following image: "I see a very clear picture of Siamese twins—the funny part of it is that they are not babies, but clearly an image of two men attached at the sides to each other, one is an old man and the other is a younger man."

The oddness of this image, so implausible in reality, evoked laughter from us both. I at once realized the connection between material that had been presented at the end of her last session and this image. However, it took her a few minutes of replaying the image in her mind before she saw the connection without any direct prompting from me. It turned out that she had been increasingly uncomfortable in recent months about the fact that her grown son and her husband, who had now joined together in a business venture, were becoming closer to each other than they had ever been before and were often excluding her from much of the rapport they shared, not only around work, but around interests in sporting events. The vividness and clarity of the image helped her suddenly to realize the extent to which she was feeling more and more like an outsider in her family, and how she would have to begin to think about finding resources within herself that would free her from her dependence on both husband and son.

This vignette demonstrates the crystallizing potential of our imagery capacity. In effect, the woman produced a kind of waking dream that represented a dramatic metaphor for her experience of increased isolation and for her envy of the increased "attachment" between father and son. She was able to formulate this into a verbal system and to recognize that resentment of the closeness between father and son was pointless.

Instead, this rapport could be welcomed as a natural development for the two men and did not automatically exclude her from full participation in the pleasures of family life. It did point up the necessity for her developing a new sense of her own role both as an individual and within the reconstructed family unit that would be appropriate to her present stage of life.

Reyher (1963) has carried the imagery association method much further within a psychoanalytic framework than any other recent clinician. He has urged the value of much more extensive periods of pure imagery association and has provided considerable research data to indicate that not only are verbalizations freer of defensiveness during such imagery-association sessions, but also that physiological indices of emotional arousal, as well as behavioral indices, support the greater "involvement" of the patient when such methods are employed. Reyher's "emergent uncovering" technique deserves more serious consideration as a regular part of ongoing psychodynamic therapies, in particular, as a method for avoiding the often excessively prolonged verbal ratiocination and defensiveness that characterize so much of the undirected psychoanalytic session.

One of the major functions of the imagery system is to permit a directness of communication between people which is often free of the excessive abstraction of verbal formulations. The so-called hovering or free-floating attention, the stance Freud advocated for the psychoanalyst during an ongoing session, seems to me to involve, at its best, an attempt to translate into images the experiences described by the patient. I believe that when the therapist is translating material from the patient into such verbal formulations as "a typical ego-superego conflict," or "obviously an early displacement of oral conflict," the therapist may be losing contact with the reality of the patient's experience. It seems much more useful for the therapist's orientation to be one of producing images that attempt, as much as possible, to concretize what it is the patient is describing. If the patient is presenting an account of a walk on the beach with an intimate friend, then the therapist's imagery ought to be in effect reproducing that walk and, in some degree, empathizing with the patient's presentation of the experience as closely as possible. Here, of course, there is the danger that the therapist, because he or she obviously draws on a different and more personal set of memories to reproduce these images, will inevitably fail to capture the patient's experience. Tauber and Green (1959) have examined this issue at some length and with considerable perceptiveness. While recognizing the dangers of countertransference and of foisting upon the patient one's own personal experiences, they also call attention to the fact that the therapist's private images may clarify the experiences going on between patient and therapist.

In one instance, as a patient of mine recounted an early childhood family scene, I tried to picture the group seated around the table. I suddenly realized from her presentation that there was a discrepancy between the number of children seated with the parents and her original account to me of how many siblings she had. One of the children was missing. When I inquired about this, she became flustered and herself tried counting, and came up with two different enumerations of her siblings. After the session, which was just ending, she went home and rethought the whole episode, experiencing a cathartic and dramatic emergence of a whole series of memories about a brother who had died. While he had been lying very sick, she had been playing with her ball against the side of the house and her grandmother had emerged from the back door to shout at her angrily, "Do you want to be the death of your brother?"

In some instances, as Tauber and Green have pointed out, the therapist may generate a completely original fantasy or daydream that may be in itself revealing of something the patient is implicitly communicating, or of a difficulty in the interaction between patient and therapist. In one instance, as a patient was engaged in free association, I became aware of a vivid image in my own mind of a Galapogos Island tortoise lumbering along on a sandy shore. After thinking about the image for a little while, I finally interrupted the patient to convey this to him, and between ourselves we quickly recognized that he had been extremely defensive during the earlier part of the session and was trying to avoid coming to grips with a particularly difficult and embarrassing situation that had occurred recently.

The imagery system, as I have suggested already, is closely related to artistic and often humorous expression. Within the psychoanalytic session, a more direct use of imagery may help not only the therapist but the patient recognize the creative potential that we all share in this medium. As a matter of fact, patients have often remarked about the fact that, despite the belief they hold at the outset that they rarely dream, once encouraged to do so by a psychoanalyst, they are surprised at how many dreams do occur and at how interesting they turn out to be. If anything, one of the real dangers of psychoanalysis as a form of clinical intervention is the fact that the inherent, somewhat narcissistic interest we all take in our own dreams and fantasies may become the basis for a continuously reinforcing experience in its own right.

Thus, people will continue to attend psychoanalytic treatment for years and years, finding the sessions themselves worthwhile and enjoyable even though there is very little evidence that they have made important gains in the form of improved interpersonal relationships or major symptom relief outside of the sessions.

At certain times in an ongoing treatment process the occurrence of a vivid image may help both therapist and patient re-examine their relationship and move to a new level of mutual understanding. In one instance a patient had spent quite a number of sessions with me talking on and on, producing boring material. I experienced the sessions, as I thought about them, much as someone who has no investments must experience the daily news report of stock exchange transactions. It occurred to me that it might be useful to the patient to discontinue this approach for awhile and instead attempt to produce a series of inter-related images. I was not too hopeful that this extremely pedestrian and boring individual would do anything. It was fascinating that almost immediately the patient began to unreel a series of images which included some rather vivid scenes of Japanese Samurai warriors engaged in combat. When we examined these images further together, it became clear that this man actually had a much more elaborate and vivid imagery capacity than either of us had realized. Of course, the suppressed anger and the desire for a more heroic life stance were also apparent. What was especially useful, however, was the fact that suddenly both patient and therapist became more interested in the transaction between them, and the patient became more excited about his own inner life as a resource.

In still another instance, a woman patient who had had a fairly extended psychotherapy history over the years kept talking at great length about a whole series of physical symptoms. Session after session she described her various frustrations in getting appropriate specialists to take her symptoms seriously. I suggested to this young woman that we try a form of the European imagery trip—imagining herself in a field or in a forest and producing a whole series of images, one after another, from such a beginning. To my surprise, once she had practiced this a little by using the Jacobsen progressive relaxation technique and some other imagery exercises as a kind of "warmup," she suddenly launched on an extremely elaborate series of images. As she did so, it became clear that she was a person who had a highly refined and sensitive awareness of nature, of colors, shapes, and sounds, and indeed a fine esthetic sense that carried over to artistic appreciation as well. This experience greatly enlivened the interaction between us, for each of us now saw how much personal richness and potential was being suppressed by her defensive preoccupation with symptomatology.

It should be apparent that I am stressing here the structural characteristics of imagery and their relation to broader self-awareness, empathy, and positive affect. Of course, psychoanalytic approaches have traditionally emphasized the content implications of the images produced, that is to say, their relation to the dynamics of early childhood conflicts, and so on. Without minimizing the importance of some of those findings, what I am trying to underline is that images are too easily overlooked as a major ego function and resource for effective coping. Although the working-through process in psychoanalysis has often in effect helped patients develop their imagery capacities, this has rarely been recognized systematically by writers on psychoanalytic technique. It can be argued that psychoanalysis in its very method provides a form of training so that the patient eventually can carry on the following kind of process.

A young man walks into a crowded room and suddenly finds himself feeling extremely uncomfortable and particularly annoyed at one person who seems to be holding forth in a small group. Whereas in the past he might have either left the room at once or perhaps gotten into the group and ended up in an argument with this man, he has now learned instead to carry out in effect an "instant replay" of his series of perceptions and thoughts as he walked into the room. By doing so, he is able to recognize that his feeling of distress was occasioned by a superficial resemblance between the other man and his own stepfather who had recurrently humiliated him about his intellectual attainments when he was a boy. He now has a system for coping with a variety of sudden irrational feelings that in the past had erupted into impulsive action which he would later regret.

I should like to stress the fact that imagery can often become a part of a more general set of private cognitions and coping skills. Psychoanalysts often notice that patients in a sense adopt the therapist as a kind of imaginary companion, someone to whom they talk privately in their minds when confronted with difficult situations. This pattern of behavior need not be viewed necessarily as an instance of excessive attachment or dependency. Often it is a natural phase of a new learning procedure in which the patient is gradually assimilating what in effect the analyst has been teaching him about a process of self-examination and heightened self-awareness. In the successful analysis, the image of the therapist should gradually fade and the function of self-examination become a much more automatic, ego-syntonic process. If we recognize the naturalness of this process, we need not be afraid to suggest it actively from time to time in order to help the patient use his or her imagery capacities to deal with potentially threatening or frightening situations. In some instances I have encouraged patients who had particular sets of fears or anxieties about particular encounters or travel to imagine that I was along with them, or that they were writing me a letter describing a set of events. This method turned out to be useful not only in helping them to deal with the stress as it occurred, but also in helping them to formulate some of the nature of the difficulty and to suggest some alternative strategies for dealing with the situation.

This orientation, while it has come out of more psychodynamically oriented treatment procedures, bears comparison with the newer developments in what has been called cognitive behavior modification and the recent emphasis on shorter term intervention procedures oriented toward self-regulation and self-control (Meichenbaum, 1977; Schwartz & Shapiro, 1976–1977). Meichenbaum (1977), for example, has proposed that:

> Therapeutic change comes about by means of a sequential, mediating process, in which (1) the client becomes aware of his maladaptive intra- and interpersonal behavior; (2) this self-recognition is the occasion for the client to emit a set of incompatible images and self-statements and incompatible behavior; (3) finally, what the client says to himself (i.e., his appraisals, attributions, self-statements, and images), following the emission of a new behavioral act and its accompanying consequences, will influuence the nature and stability of the change. As far as we, as therapists, can *anticipate* and *subsume* the content of the client's internal dialogue in our treatment package, we will be that much more effective. [p. 224].

Important differences in objectives remain between the psychodynamic approaches, which place considerable emphasis on early origin and on a dynamic causal analysis for adult emotional problems, and the newer cognitive behavior modification methods, which focus primarily on a more immediate analysis of maladaptive behavior patterns. Still, it is important to see that both approaches are making increased use of imagery in helping to formulate information about the nature of the dilemma the patient brings, and also in providing some clear-cut tools to the therapist for, in effect, retraining the patient's capacity for coping as well as self-understanding.

Within the psychodynamic tradition, it seems to me there is increasing room for more active use of imagery approaches. Shorr (1972) has developed a series of ingenious imagery "assignments" to help the patient to concretize an array of interpersonal dilemmas and also to identify existential difficulties. Leuner (1969) has made use of the guided imagery method in a systematic fashion to uncover major motivational difficulties. By having a patient engage in an imagery trip with respect to climbing a mountain, one can get clues to problems in relation to ambitions, power strivings, and so on. By having the patient engage in an imagery trip related to following a stream to its source, one can often gain important clues through imagery about the relation of child to mother and some sense of important early experiences of attachment. In effect, the range of uses of imagery is almost unlimited, once the patient comes to accept this dimension of cognition as an adaptive resource and not simply as a form of regressive experience.

Uses of Imagery in More Direct Forms of Clinical Intervention

It is intriguing that the many forms of short-term clinical intervention which have developed in the last 15 years, largely as reactions against the length and limited application of psychoanalysis or other personality-change psychodynamic therapies, have increasingly relied on private experience as a critical feature of the treatment. Wolpe's systematic desensitization, perhaps the most effective and certainly the most thoroughly researched of current behavior therapy approaches, turns out eventually to rely primarily on the patient's production of private imagery rather than on his or her overt behavior (Wilkins 1971). Thus, behaviorism, which grew up as a reaction against the introspective orientation of psychology at the turn of the century, has led back again to considerable concern with the nature of human imagery and of private events, as opposed to directly observable stimulus-response connections. Indeed, the recent reviews of basic literature on the technique of systematic desensitization have made it clear that the critical factor in treatment is not so much the hierarchy with its ordering of least-to-most phobic situations, or the use of the progressive relaxaion. Instead, the most significant feature again and again turns out to be the imagery used by the patient. What is becoming increasingly clear is that for many phobias—the symptom for which systematic desensitization is most effective—the thought of fear about the situation prevents the individual from ever coming anywhere near the phobic object or situation and, therefore, from ever finding out that it can indeed be tolerated. Once one can, through a series of images, gradually attend to the situation and try it out in a variety of imagined settings, then an actual real life approach becomes much more possible, with the frequent consequence that the phobia disappears rather quickly.

Recent research (Kazdin, 1976) has also made it clear that we still do not understand fully the critical "ingredient" in the effectiveness of systematic desensitization. At least some studies that have used credible placebo or "bogus therapeutic" strategies have obtained equally good results. Again, such findings suggest that a critical factor in such a treatment is not the conditioning effect but, much more probably, a change in the private anticipations, in the images, self-communication, and daydreams that the patient holds with respect to the critical situations for which treatment has been sought.

There is also increasing evidence that while direct experience, or what is often called *in vivo* treatment, is often most effective, the difference between such treatments and the imagined experience is not so great. Therefore, a good deal more may actually be accomplished in the limited psychotherapeutic setting through the use of extended imagery, and this imagery may indeed be generalized when carefully carried out and associated with additional cognitions and related coping skills.

Behavior modifiers and cognitive behavior therapists are also making increasing use of aversive control techniques. The patient imagines extremely noxious and unpleasant outcomes for certain situations and rehearses these again and again so that when the thought of engaging in an unwanted or antisocial action comes to mind, the patient quickly introduces the unpleasant consequences of such an act and often is deterred from engaging in it. If a set of instructive alternative images is also provided for the patient, with his or her gaining some support through experiencing rewards in imagery for such behavior, a considerable flexibility can be generated.

In one instance, a patient with whom I worked was attempting to control a personally unacceptable tendency to anonymous homosexual pickups. By the use of a variety of extremely noxious images, he gradually, but rather quickly, gave up this long-term compulsive pattern. He also rewarded himself mentally by imagining successful encounters of a more fully developed nature with women. Eventually, and rather rapidly considering his long history of anonymous homosexual behavior, he moved into a much more complex and satisfying heterosexual relationship that led to a satisfactory marriage. In this instance, while I had worked out at some length with him through more traditional analytic methods the dynamics underlying this problem, the compulsive behavior was not altered until we introduced a systematic, aversive-imagery procedure.

An extensive and carefully researched literature exists on what might be called vicarious or symbolic modeling techniques following the procedures pioneered by Bandura (1977). Bandura has been able to demonstrate that imagining other persons who engage successfully in either acts of freedom from phobia or acts of self-control from unwanted impulsive behavior, and are reinforced socially or psychologically for such actions, can generalize in the individual patient to effective behavior later on. Again, one sees the possibility that all too often individuals have developed longstanding patterns of self-defeating action and, because of their anxiety or often because of limited actual experience, have not been able to anticipate alternative approaches to coping with these behaviors. Indeed Meichenbaum and Turk (1975) have pointed out that often, even when patients do prove capable of imagining alternative successful coping behaviors, they lack a systematic set of self-instructions to sustain them as they engage in the activity. Meichenbaum (1974) has developed a whole set of self-instruction techniques designed for what he calls "stress inoculation." These methods use a combination of verbal self-statements as well as images designed to help a person get through particular stressful situations or, anticipating these situations, to carry out what Janis (1968) has called the "work of worrying" to establish an effective coping strategy. Within these procedures, considerable stress is placed on the individual's ability to use imagery to distract him- or herself, to shift attention, or to generate very strong experiences that might be capable of psychophysiological counteraction. In a series of ingenious studies, Turk (1977) has shown that individuals can sustain a remarkable amount of pain by the use of images, among other kinds of self-cognitions, that provide alternative "contexts" or may actually lead to biofeedback that inhibits the pain response.

The effectiveness of imagery in a host of self-regulation procedures is increasingly being recognized. I myself have encouragd patients who seem to be caught in moderate depressive cycles to use images of peaceful nature scenes or related positive events to see whether these can change the mood, at least temporarily, and therefore permit the patient to engage in more effective behavior that may break up the snowballing effect of the depressed affect. Recently, Schultz (1976) has carried out extensive research demonstrating that severely depressed, hospitalized male patients who engage either in self-esteem-enhancing imagery or in imagery of positive nature scenes can reduce the amount of depression and actually show a greater capacity for laughter and positive emotion. It is of interest to note that Schultz's imagery methods were also differentially effective depending on the patient's depressive style. For those patients who had depressive symptomatology related more to early experiences of loss of love and lowered self-esteem, the self-esteem-enhancing imagery was more effective. For patients whose depression was more related to superego conflicts, the focus on positive imagery as a distractor turned out to be more useful. Contrary to theories that depression is introjected aggression, aggressive fantasies themselves do not necessarily reduce the depression for the superego-conflict patients. Instead, the distraction and positive affect associated with peaceful nature scenes seemed to be more effective.

Imagery has, of course, been increasingly used to enhance sexual arousal. Despite early beliefs that fantasy and daydreaming represent forms of drive reduction, it is increasingly clear that imagery provides a context for increasing sexual arousal, and that this can be especially effective in helping individuals overcome particular types of sexual difficulties (Hariton and Singer, 1974; Kaplan, 1974; J.L. Singer, 1975b). It should be noted that in the newly evolving multimodal therapeutic orientation of Lazarus (1975), in Ellis's rational-emotive therapy (1973), as well as in other recent short-term intervention techniques, there has been increasing emphasis on systematic training of patients in awareness and use of their own imagery for dealing with a variety of interpersonal behaviors, as well as sexuality.

A recent experiment by Frank (1977) under my direction demonstrated rather clearly that young adults, given opportunities to become more aware of their own ongoing imagery capacities by maintaining logs of night dreams and sharing with each other (without interpretation) their night and daydreams, became increasingly more empathic as measured by a variety of objective procedures. That is, they were subsequently (in comparison with various control groups) more capable of identifying the implicit meanings in others' communications and of recognizing emotions expressed through facial or verbal gesture by others and on the whole became more sensitive to the affective dimension of human experience.

In general, a growing body of evidence. indicates that systematic application of imagery methods can be effective in treating a variety of established neurotic conditions; in improving interpersonal behavior, such as lack of assertiveness or shyness; in treating sexual difficulties; in helping individuals control weight; and in treating socially undesirable behaviors, such as excessive drinking or antisocial activities and impulsivity. We are still at the beginning in this area in terms of identifying specific facets of imagery that are more or less effective, identifying those individuals who are more or less capable of different degrees of imagery, and developing techniques for enhancing imagery capacities (J.L. Singer, 1975).

Self-Efficacy and Imagery

I have suggested that one of the major recurring themes in all uses of imagery in psychotherapy or behavior modification is that of the sense of self-control the patient gains because imagery is so private (J.L. Singer, 1974). Bandura (1976, 1977a, 1977b), in developing his theory of social learning, has increasingly emphasized cognitive processes and the importance of self-efficacy in producing ultimate behavior change. He has argued that psychological procedures, such as the various psychotherapies or presumably approaches involving persuasion or placebo suggestion, essentially provide the individual with means of strengthening private imagery of "expectations of self-efficacy" (Bandura, 1977c). Translating Bandura's formal (and formidable) language, our projections into the future involve the outcomes we can expect from certain actions and also our images or self-verbalizations of whether we can successfully carry out the necessary actions to produce such outcomes. This approach represents a revival of Lewin's (1935) early emphasis on "means-end cognizance," a concept employed long ago to analyze fantasy projections of various social classes or pathological groups (J.L. Singer and Sugarman, 1955). Self-efficacy cognitions in the form of imagery, fantasies, or self-communications in some form determine whether we will initiate certain types of behavior and, once engaged in them, how long we will persist or how much effort we will expend. The private image that one can cope will help one stick it out in situations that are believed to be dangerous, embarrassing, or otherwise aversive. Such persistence often pays off in the sense that one finds one can indeed handle such situations, and therefore it strengthens a sense of self-efficacy.

One can see in the increased emphasis on self-constructs in social learning and cognitive style theories (Witkin and Goodenough, 1976) some potential integration with psychodynamic theories. In psychoanalysis, for example, the concept of introjected parental figures or ego ideals serves as a key to a kind of private self-reinforcement or symbolic modeling that steers our behavior. Bandura's approach carries these notions a step or two further along toward an operational formulation of the components of private experience that contribute to self-efficacy or self-reinforcement (Bandura, 1976, 1977a, 1977b). We need to be able to assess systematically the magnitude, generality and strength of our expectations of how well we can cope with situations. Our expectations themselves are based on what we actually have accomplished and our observations of how well others we know have done in similar situations, for example, our parents or siblings. They also depend on suggestions from others which are more or less persuasive, for example, a placebo effect which leads us to believe that the addition of a certain drug to our body's armamentarium or the completion of a particular type of psychotherapy will make us more capable of coping with hitherto frightening or difficult circumstances. Indeed, verbal persuasion may also operate to change our attitude when we perceive logical fallacies in our own beliefs, a principle central to Ellis's rational-emotional psychotherapy. Such effects are also evident in psychoanalysis where "insight" often means a patient's recognition that a longstanding belief or behavior pattern represents the persistence in adult life of a childhood misunderstanding, inept parental "suggestion," or immature fantasy. An insight of such a type may lead to a change in the patient's image of potential future coping capacities. In transactional terms the patient may be able to say, "I no longer have to play the buffoon or *schlemiel* to get along with others at work—I can get their interest and respect by just doing my work well."

The feedback effects of emotional arousal must also be considered in a theory of self-efficacy. Actual participation in frightening or unpleasant situations leaves a memory of the negative affect experience. Sometimes, even without an actual aversive or failure experience, a person's lack of belief in coping skills for dealing with such situations may lead to strong negative affect just in imagining such situations. Such methods as systematic desensitization, implosive therapy, or symbolic modeling often lead people to recognize that they can reduce the negative affect associated with imagined situations and provide them with an additional sense that they have coping skills if they confront such situations in reality.

One's self-efficacy orientation is strongly related to chronic affective conditions, such as depression. The research and intervention strategies of Beck (1967) and Seligman (1975) emphasize the long-term sense of helplessness or the beliefs that one lacks any efficacy for coping. Very likely we can become depressed if we have experienced a series of failures (or if our parents have early in life convinced us that we have) and therefore cannot generate imagery of any positive outcomes in our lives. For example, Starker and Singer (1975) found that depressed patients had fewer daydreams of a pleasant, wishful character than did other psychiatric patients. A recent study by Rizley (1976) suggests that depressed college students are more likely to be precise in attending to their actual failures or limited attainments while non-depressed individuals tend somewhat to overestimate their achievements or possibilities. Hope and fantasied efficacy, if not too unrealistic, may sustain performance and avoid the debilitating effects of depressive mood.

It seems likely that our capacity for considering multiple possibilities through imagery may be strengthened by certain types of psychotherapy. Having learned to use imagery, we can now add it to our repertoire of coping skills. The awareness of these skills adds to the specific sense of efficacy we experience in relation to particular upcoming situations. It remains to be seen whether one can talk of a generalized sense of personal efficacy, a position Bandura would question, or at least whether we can differentiate between individuals in terms of the range of situations they will probably confront and their personal sense of possessing coping skills for each of these—a kind of quantitative measure of ego strength.

SOME PREVENTIVE AND CONSTRUCTIVE USES OF OUR IMAGERY CAPACITIES

I should like to conclude by briefly pointing to some of the preventive or constructive day-to-day implications of imagery, as I see them. Here we have to move somewhat further away from extensive research evidence, although there is mounting support from formal research for many of the points I shall make.

Imagery for Healthy Escapism

Too often our tendencies to daydreaming and fantasy have been labeled as harmful because they have served as forms of escape from the rigors of day-to-day life or from the challenge of direct interpersonal interaction. There seems no question that many of us do indeed use our images or fantasies for such maladaptive escapist purposes. That recognition, however, has often led people to an excessive concern with the more negative aspects of their daydreaming or imaginative capacities (J.L. Singer, 1975b). As a matter of fact there are many situations in which a kind of healthy escapism may be the most useful method of dealing with the reality that faces us. On a long train ride, in a waiting-room situation, in a variety of social settings in which we are powerless to act to change our situation, the shift of attention from the dangers or rigors of the immediate setting or its boredom, for that matter, may actually help pass the time and may avoid our developing emotional and, indeed, psychophysiological reactions (Schwartz and Shapiro, 1976, 1978) that may be self-defeating.

Some people suffer from insomnia because of concerns about actions that they need to take the following day but that they are powerless to accomplish the night before. Probably the best way of getting to sleep is to develop a recurring and moderately elaborate fantasy that is sufficiently interesting to distract one from the unfinished business of one's life, and yet not so engrossing as to prevent the natural sleep processes from occurring. Some people have found that imagining themselves engaging in ballet or in sports activities has worked especially effectively from this standpoint. Thus, we can find a great many simple uses for our capacity to engage in attitudes toward the possible, or even the impossible, with impunity via our imagery modality.

Imagery Uses for Self-Awareness

Perhaps more than any other human process, imagery is uniquely our own. In this sense we can use our capacities for playful shifts of focus, combinations of characters, recall of pleasant vacations, or anticipation of pleasant trips in the future to help us not only to escape, but also to learn something more about the things that have seemed to be of special value. Keeping a log of one's night dreams or one's daydreams and then examining these for recurring themes, such as interest in power, achievement, sexual fulfillment, concern for others, understanding others, understanding nature, and avoiding frightening situations, all can provide us eventually with a kind of patterning of our own major motivational structure. Even beyond this we can begin to find out more and more about the range of roles we might like to play.

We may also gain an awareness about the nature of creativity or inner playfulness itself. To what extent can we, in reading a book, become so immersed in the set of events that we find ourselves almost unable to switch back our attention. This kind of absorption, which in many ways is closely related to the intense imagery that characterizes the hypnotic state, may also tell us a good deal about our desires for deeper experience and for freeing ourselves from some of the superficialities of day-to-day interchange.

It is obvious, of course, that our fantasies will also reveal many of our more petty or less socially desirable tendencies: our jealousies, our envies of the success of others, our hatreds and prejudices. Here again, recognizing the strengths and limitations of one's imagery dimension can help one cope with these. Most white people in our society will quickly recognize, whether through dreams or daydream images, some of their latent prejudice against colored minorities. We may surprise ourselves sometimes, despite our liberal front, by noticing such tendencies. At the same time, however, we need not be overwhelmed by guilt. We are, after all, reflecting a tremendous range of cultural experience in our thoughts and fantasies. The awareness of such tendencies may alert us more effectively to the way in which such prejudices may eventually work their way into behavior, and we may then avoid such actions more effectively.

Imagery for Self-Regulation and Biofeedback

It is increasingly clear that a major dimension of human variation has to do with the degree to which individuals have learned a variety of skills for what may be called self-regulation or self-control. Indeed, Strupp (1970) has argued that the major implication of the various forms of psychotherapy has to do with the degree to which individuals learn to control their emotions or their impulsive activity. In many ways the use of our imagery turns out to be a major form of self-control. By trying out in imagery, actions we may undertake in the future, we can learn the possibilities and limitations of such actions. We may use imagery, as has been suggested in the previous section to control negative affects or to enhance positive experiences or sexual enjoyment. Imagery is something that is very much within our control and no one else's, and in this sense it has special advantages. In addition, we are increasingly clear that our own fully developed images are not simply pure "mind" acts. They are integrally related to ongoing bodily processes and, indeed, may have feedback consequences, as the work of Schwartz and Shapiro (1976, 1978) demonstrates. A growing body of research in the field of behavioral medicine suggests that important approaches to the treatment of physical disease, such as hypertension, may involve systematic use of imagery and related techniques for reducing blood pressure or modifying other physically maladaptive behaviors.

Imagery thus has a tremendous range of possibilities in the area of self-control and development. Work being carried out in the field of sports suggests that systematic mental practice through visualization and fantasy may actually lead to improved functioning in athletic contests. Football players, for instance, O.J. Simpson (New Haven Register, 1976), report that they have made important gains in their own playing style through the use of mental anticipation. A series of researches by Richardson (1969) and by Suinn (1976) has also indicated the clear advantages to athletes of mental practice. We have probably not carried this far enough in the area of social role rehearsal. Increasing concern about enhancing our ability for effective social interaction, techniques of assertiveness training, and techniques of more effective role sharing in men and women all involve anticipatory imagery. We need not fear the future so much if we allow ourselves to play out a variety of scenarios and then gradually choose the one that seems most reasonable, keeping in mind that with each actual experience we can re-examine our options.

Imagery for Esthetic and Creative Development

The dimension of imagery, as I have suggested many times, is close to the highest levels of human achievement in the arts. When we read a story, our ability to immerse ourselves almost totally in the framework of the author and to travel with him or her into a far-off country provides us with a whole series of images and pictures that not only will we enjoy in the reading itself but that will continue to be played and replayed in our minds. It is not only the actual esthetic experience, but the memory of it and then the anticipation that enhance the value of our art. If the television medium is to be faulted from an esthetic standpoint, it is largely because its rapidity of presentation holds one's attention almost completely on the set and leaves little room for imagery and fantasy. Reading, radio, or the theater allow more leeway in this respect.

Our ability to immerse ourselves in characters of other people gives us, in an odd way, a chance to lead many lives in the short space of our own limited journey on this planet. We need not be afraid that we will become schizophrenics if we develop a set of alter egos from literature or art or the opera. Instead, we may enhance the flexibility and fluidity of our lives. Naturally, one cannot withdraw from day-to-day meaningful social encounter in such experiences. However, often we may draw on these alternate dimensions to sustain us or to enlarge our perspective on the meaning of our own lives.

In its own way, because of its range of possibilities, fantasy is also close to humor. We can stand situations on their heads and startle ourselves from time to time with the novelty of our inventiveness. In doing so, we may laugh as we realize this novelty still remains our own private fiction. Indeed, as we allow ourselves this range of fantasy possibility, we may appreciate the outlandish humor of a Donald Barthelme or a Woody Allen.

Religion, prayer, and philosophy may be concretized for us in a variety of ways and may be used, similarly, to deepen our sense of relationship, and also occasionally to provide us with the additional leaven of humor. I sometimes like to think of ourselves as walking through life toward the setting sun much as in the fadeout of a Chaplin movie. As one heads toward that distant horizon, it may be fun, once in a while in imagery, to flip a little side kick or a hitch of our belt as Charlie used to do, a gesture that adds just that extra touch of humor and modesty to the journey.

REFERENCES

Bandura, A. (1976), Effecting change through participant modeling. In: *Counseling Methods*, ed. J.D. Krumboltz & C.E. Thoresen. New York: Holt, Rinehart & Winston.

————— (1976), Self-reinforcement: Theoretical and methodological considerations, *Behaviorism*, 4:135–155.

————— (1977a), *Social Learning Theory*. Englewood Cliffs, N.J.: Prentice Hall.

————— (1977b), Self-efficacy: Towards a unifying theory of behavioral change. *Psychol. Rev.*, 84:191–215.

Beck, A.T. (1967), *Depression*. New York: Harper & Row

Biblow, E. (1973), Imaginative play and the control of aggressive behavior. In: *The Child's World of Make-Believe*, ed. J.L. Singer. New York: Academic Press.

Bogen, J.E. (1969), The other side of the brain. *Bull. Los Angeles Neurol. Soc.* 34:135–162.

Bourne, L.E., Ekstrand, B.R., & Dominowski, R.L. (1971), *The Psychology of Thinking*. Englewood Cliffs, N.J.: Prentice-Hall.

Desoille, R. (1961), *Théorie et Pratique du Rêve Eveillé Dirigé*. Geneva: Mont-Blanc.

Eisenstein, S. (1942), *The Film Sense*. New York: Harcourt Brace.

Ekman, P., Friesen, W.V., & Ellsworth, P. (1971), *Emotions in the Human Face: Guidelines for Research and a Review of Findings*. New York: Pergamon.

Eliot, T.S. (1950), Hamlet and his problems. In: *Selected Essays*. New York: Harcourt Brace.

Ellis, A. (1973), The no cop-out theory. *Psychol. Today*, 7:56–60.

Fein, G. (1975), A transformational analysis of pretending. *Devel. Psychol.*, 11:291–296.

Fein, G. & Robertson, A. (1974), Cognitive and social dimensions of play in two-year-olds. Mimeographed Report, Yale University.

Feitelson, D. (1972), Developing imaginative play in pre-school children as a possible approach to fostering creativity. *Early Child Devel. & Care*, 1:181–195.

———— & Ross, G.S. (1973), The neglected factor—play. *Human Devel.* 16: 202–223.

Ferenczi, S. (1950), *Sex in Psychoanalysis.* New York: Basic Books.

Frank, S.J. (1977), The facilitation of empathy through training in imagination. Unpublished doctoral dissertation, Yale University.

Franklin, D. (1975), Block play modeling and its relationship to imaginativenes, impulsivity-reflection and internal-external control. Unpublished predissertation research, Yale University.

Freud, S. (1962), *The Interpretation of Dreams.* In: *The Standard Edition of the Complete Psychological Works.* Vols. 4 & 5, ed. J. Strachey. London: Hogarth.

Freyberg, J.T. (1973), Increasing the imaginative play of urban disadvantaged kindergarten children through systematic training. In: *The Child's World of Make-Believe,* ed. J.L. Singer. New York: Academic Press.

Gazzaniga, H.S. (1967), The split brain in man. *Sci. Amer.* 217:24–29.

Gill, M. (1963), *Topography and Systems in Psychoanalytic Theory* [*Psychol. Issues*, Monograph 10]. New York: International Universities Press.

Gottlieb, S. (1973), Modeling effects upon fantasy. In: *The Child's World of Make-Believe,* ed. J.L. Singer. New York: Academic Press.

Hariton, E.B. & Singer, J.L. (1974), Women's fantasies during sexual intercourse: Normative and theoretical implications. *J. Consult. Clin. Psychol.*

Holt, R. (1964), Imagery: The return of the ostracized. *Amer. Psychol.* 19: 254–264.

Horowitz, M.J. (1970), *Image Formation and Cognition.* New York: Appleton-Century-Crofts.

———— (1975), Intrusive and repetitive thought after experimental stress. *Arch. Gen. Psychiat.* 32:1457–1463.

Izard, C.E. (1971), *The Face of Emotion.* New York: Appleton-Century-Crofts.

———— (1977), *Human Emotions.* New York: Plenum.

James, W. (1890), *The Principles of Psychology,* 2 vols. New York: Dover, (1950).

Janis, I.L. (1968), Human reactions to stress. In: *Handbook of Personality Theory and Research,* ed. E. Borgotta & W. Lambert. New York: Rand-McNally.

Jaynes, J. (1977), *The Origin of Consciousness in the Breakdown of the Bicameral Mind.* Boston: Houghton-Mifflin.

Johnson, D.M. (1955), *The Psychology of Thought and Judgment.* New York: Harper & Row.

Kagan, J. & Kogan, N. (1970), Individual variation in cognitive processes. In: *Carmichael's Manual of Child Psychology,* Vol. I, ed. P. Mussen. New York: Wiley.

Kaplan, H.S. (1974), *The New Sex Therapy.* New York: Brunner/Mazel.

Kazdin, A.E. (1976), Effects of covert modeling, multiple models, and model reinforcement on assertive behavior. *Behav. Ther.* 7:211–222.

Kinsbourne, M. (1971), The control of attention by interaction between the cerebral hemispheres. Presented at the Fourth International Symposium on Attention and Performance, Boulder, Col.

———— (1973a), The control of attention by interaction between the cerebral hemispheres. In: *Attention and Performance IV,* ed. S. Kornblum. New York: Academic Press.

———— (Ed.) (1973b), *Hemispheric Asymmetry of Function.* London: Tavistock.

Kocel, K., Galin, D., Ornstein, R., & Merrin, E.L. (1972), Lateral eye movement and cognitive mode. *Psychonomic Sci.* 27:223–224.

Kohlberg, L. (1966), A cognitive-developmental approach to socialization, morality, and psychosexuality. Presented at Midwestern Meeting of the Society for Research in Child Development, Bowling Green State University, Bowling Green, Ohio.

Kris, E. (1951), On preconscious mental processes. In: *Organization and Pathology of Thought,* ed. D. Rapaport. New York: Columbia University Press.

Lazarus, A. (1971), *Behavior Therapy and Beyond.* New York: McGraw-Hill.

Leuner, H. (1969), Guided affective imagery (GAI): A method of intensive psychotherapy. *Amer. J. Psychother.* 23:4–22.

Lewin, K. (1935), *A Dynamic Theory of Personality.* New York: McGraw-Hill.

Litt, H. (1973), Imagery in children's thinking. Unpublished doctoral dissertation, Liverpool University.

Marshall, H. & Hahn, S.C. (1967), Experimental modification of dramatic play. *J. Pers. Soc. Psychol.,* 5:119–122.

Meichenbaum, D. (1974), *Cognitive Behavior Modification.* Morristown, N.J.: General Learning Press.

———— (1975), A cognitive behavior modification approach to assessment. In: *Behavioral Assessment: A Practical Handbook,* ed. M. Hersen & A. Bellack. New York: Pergamon.

———— (1977), *Cognitive-Behavior Modification: An Integrative Approach.* New York: Plenum.

———— & Turk, D. (1975), The cognitive-behavioral management of anxiety, anger and pain. In: *Proceedings of the seventh Banff international conference on behavior modification.* Research Press.

Mischel, W. (1971), *Introduction to Personality.* New York: Holt, Rinehart, & Winston.

———— (1973), Toward a cognitive social learning reconceptualization of personality. *Psychol. Rev.* 80:252–283.

———— Zeiss, R., & Zeiss, A. (1974), Internal-external control and persistence. *J. Pers. Soc. Psychol.* 29:265–278.

Morgan, A.H., McDonald, P.J., & MacDonald, H. (1971), Differences in bilateral alpha activity as a function of experimental task, with a note on lateral eye movements and hypnotizability. *Neuropsychologia,* 9:459–469.

Nahme-Huang, L., Singer, D.G., Singer, J.L., & Wheaton, A. (1977), Imaginative play and perceptual motor intervention methods with emotionally-disturbed, hospitalized children: An Evaluation Study (1977). *Amer. J. Orthopsychiat.,* 47:238–249.

New Haven Register (1976), Interview with O.J. Simpson, January.

Paivio, A. (1971), *Imagery and Verbal Processes.* New York: Holt.

Piaget, J. (1932), *The Language and Thought of the Child.* New York: Harcourt Brace.

Perls, F. (1970), *Gestalt Therapy Verbatim.* New York: Bantam Books.

Pulaski, M.A. (1973), Toys and imaginative play. In: *The Child's World of Make-Believe,* ed. J.L. Singer, New York: Academic Press.

Rapaport, D. (1951), *Organization and Pathology of Thought.* New York: Columbia University Press.

———— (1960), The psychoanalytic theory of motivation. In: *Nebraska Symposium on Motivation,* ed. M.R. Jones. Lincoln: University of Nebraska Press.

Reich, W. (1945), *Character Analysis,* 2nd ed. New York: Orgone Institute Press.

Reyher, J. (1963), Free imagery: An uncovering procedure. *J. Clin. Psychol.,* 19: 454–459.

Richardson, A. (1969), *Mental Imagery.* New York: Springer.

Riess, A. (1957), A study of some genetic behavioral correlates of human movement responses in children's Rorschach protocols. Unpublished doctoral dissertation, New York University.

Rizley, R.C. (1976), The perception of causality in depression: An attributional analysis of two cognitive theories of depression. Unpublished doctoral dissertation, Yale University.

Rodin. J. & Singer, J.L. (1976), Laterality of eye shift, reflective thought and obesity, *J. Personality,* 44:594–610.

Rohwer, W.D., Jr. (1970), Images and pictures in children's learning. *Psychol. Bull.,* 73:393–403.

Rosenberg, B. (1977), Visual responsiveness during different kinds of mental activity. Unpublished doctoral dissertation, Yale University.

Rosenthal, R. (1974), Body-talk and tone of voice: The language without words. *Psychol. Today,* 8:64–71.

Saltz, E., Dixon, D., & Johnson, J. (1976) *Training Disadvantaged Preschoolers on Various Fantasy Activities: Effects on Cognitive Functioning and Impulse Control.* (Technical Report No. 8). Detroit: Center for the Study of Cognitive Processes, Wayne State University, May.

Saltz, E. & Johnson, J. (1973), *Training for Thematic Fantasy Play in Culturally Disadvantaged Children: Preliminary Results* (Technical Report No. 3). Detroit: Center for the Study of Cognitive Processes, Wayne State University.

Schachtel, E. (1959), *Metamorphosis.* New York: Basic Books.

Schultz, K.D. (1976), The role of fantasy stimulation in the treatment of depressed psychiatric patients. Unpublished doctoral dissertation, Yale University.

Schwartz, G.E., Davidson, R.J., & Maer, F. (1975), Right hemisphere lateralization for emotion in the human brain: Interactions with cognition. *Science,* 190:286–288.

———— & Shapiro, D. (Eds.) (1975–1978), *Consciousness and Self-Regulation: Advances in Research,* Vols. I and II. New York: Plenum.

Seamon, J.G. (1972), Imagery codes and human information retrieval. *J. Experiment. Psychol.* 96:468–470.

Segal, S.J. (Ed.) (1971), *Imagery: Current Cognitive Approaches.* New York: Academic Press.

Seidman, J.M. (Ed.) (1960), *The Adolescent. A book of Readings,* rev. ed. New York: Holt, Reinhart, & Winston.

Seligman, M.E.P. (1975), *Helpness.* San Francisco: Freeman.

Selman, R. (1975), The development of social-cognitive understanding: A guide to educational and clinical practice. In: *Morality: Theory, Research, and Social Issues,* ed. T. Lickona. New York: Holt, Rinehart, & Winston.

Sheehan, P.W. (1972), *The Function and Nature of Imagery.* New York: Academic Press.

Shepherd, R. (1967), Recognition memory for words, sentences, and pictures. *J. Verbal Learn. Verbal Behav.* 6:156–163.

Shorr, J.E. (1972), *Psycho-Imagination Therapy.* New York: Intercontinental Medical Book Corporation.

Singer, D.G. & Singer, J.L. (1977), *Partners in Play.* New York: Harper & Row.

Singer, J.L. (1960), The experience type: Some behavioral correlates and theoretical implications. In: *Rorschach Psychology,* ed. M.R. Rickers-Ovsiankina. New York: Wiley.

———— (1961), Imagination and waiting ability in young children. *J. Pers.* 29:396–413.

———— (1966), *Daydreaming.* New York: Random House.

————— (1973), *The Child's World of Make-Believe: Experimental Studies of Imaginative Play*. New York: Academic Press.

————— (1974), *Imagery and Daydreaming Methods in Psychotherapy and Behavior Modification*. New York: Academic Press.

————— (1975a), Navigating the stream of consciousness: Research in daydreaming and related inner experience. *Amer. Psychol.*

————— (1975b), *The Inner World of Daydreaming*. New York: Harper & Row.

————— (1977), Imaginative play and pretending in early childhood: Some educational implications. *J. Ment. Imagery*, 1:127–144.

————— & Opler, M.K. (1956), Contrasting patterns of fantasy and motility in Irish and Italian schizophrenics. *J. Abnorm. Soc. Psychol.* 53: 42–47.

————— & Singer, D.G. (1976), Imaginative play and pretending in early childhood. In: *Child Personality and Psychopathology*, Vol. 3, ed. A. Davids. New York: Wiley.

————— & Sugarman, D. (1955), Some Thematic Apperception Test correlates of Rorschach human movement responses. *J. Consult. Psychol.* 19: 117–119.

————— Wilensky, H., & McCraven, V. (1956), Delaying capacity, fantasy and planning ability: A factorial study of some basic ego functions. *J. Consult. Psychol.* 20: 375–383.

Smilansky, S. (1968), *The Effects of Sociodramatic Play on Disadvantaged Preschool Children*. New York: Wiley.

Sperry, R. (1968), Hemisphere disconnection and unity in conscious awareness. *Amer. Psychol.* 23:723–733.

Spivack, G. & Levine, M. *Self-Regulation and Acting-Out in Normal Adolescents*. Progress Report for National Institute of Mental Health Grant M-4531. Devon, Pa.: Devereaux Foundation.

Starker, S. & Singer, J.L. (1975), Daydream patterns and self-awareness in psychiatric patients. *J. Nerv. Ment. Dis.*, 161:313–317.

Strupp, H.H. (1970), Specific vs. non-specific factors in psychology and the problem of control. *Arch. Gen. Psychiat.*, 23:393–401.

Suinn, R.M. (1976), Body thinking. Psychology for Olympic champs. *Psychol. Today*, 10:38–43.

Sullivan, H.S. (1956), *Clinical Studies in Psychiatry*. New York: Norton.

Sutton-Smith, B. (1975), Children's narrative competence: The underbelly of mythology. Presented at Symposium on Structure and Content in Play, American Psychological Association, Chicago.

Tauber, E.S. & Green, M.G. (1959), *Prelogical Experience*. New York: Basic Books.

Tomkins, S. (1962–1963), *Affect, Imagery, and Consciousness*, Vol. I & II. New York: Springer.

Torrance, E.P. (1966), *Torrance Tests of Creative Thinking. Verbal, Forms A & B*. Princeton, N.J.: Personnel Press.

Tucker, J. (1975), The role of fantasy in cognitive-affective functioning: Does reality make a difference in remembering? Unpublished doctoral dissertation, Teachers College, Columbia University.

Turk, D. (1977), A multimodal skills training approach to the control of experimentally produced pain. Unpublished doctoral dissertation, University of Waterloo.

Wallach, M. (1971), *The Intelligence/Creativity Distinction.* New York: General Learning Press.

Wheeler, J. (1969), Fantasy, affect, and the preception of time. Unpublished doctoral dissertation, City University of New York.

Wilkins, W. (1971), Desensitization: Social and cognitive factors underlying the effectiveness of Wolpe's procedure. *Psychol. Bull.* 76:311–317.

Wilson, E. (1922), Review of *Ulysses. New Republic,* 3:164.

Witkin, H.A. & Goodenough, D.R. (1976), Field dependence revisited. *Research Bulletin,* Princeton, New Jersey: Educational Testing Service.

Woolf, V. (1953), Modern fiction. In: *The Common Reader.* New York: Harcourt, Brace, p. 54.

Subject Index

"Activity affects", 83
Adaptational, 36
Admit, 23
Adolescence, 8, 9
Amnesia, 73, 77
Anxiety, 7, 8, 24, 34
Attachment, 83, 88
  ethologic, 84
  human, 81
Bad
  me, 25, 85
  mother, 85
  relationships, 85
Brain Information Service, 65
Circadian, 72
Cognition, 24, 27
Concretization, 19
Constancy of relationship, 86, 90
"Context-dependent", 53
Countertransference, 66
Daydreaming, 105, 109
Defense, 7
Denial, 10
Depression, 5
Detachment, 24, 81, 82, 88 89, 92, 102
Discourse, 52
Divergent thinking, 117
Dreams, 53, 66
Ecrits: A Selection, 36
Ego, 33, 39
  psychology, 33, 44
"Embeddedness affects", 83
"Emergent uncovering", 129
Enuresis, 72
  nocturnal, 74
Equifinality, 60

Ethologic, 83
Experience, 35, 52
Externalization, 20
Fantasy, 104
Free associations, 2, 36, 55, 56
Fugue states, 65, 72, 74, 77
General Systems Theory, 60, 62
Good
  me, 85
  mother, 85
  relationship, 85
Hallucinations, 20
Hostility, 24
Human
  attachment, 81, 88
  relatedness, 81
Humilliation, 96
Hypersomnia, 72
Hypochondriasis, 42
Id, 33
Identical predicates, 18
  subjects, 18
Imagery, 110, 138
Imagination, 105
"Inauthentic", 34
Indoctrination, 48
Inner self, 16
Insomnia, 72
Integrative activity, 17
Interpretation, 50, 58
Interpretation of Schizophrenia, 17
Intrapsychic representation, 83
Left brain/right brain, 61
Le Rêve Eveillé Dirigé, 125
Listening attitude, 21
Malevolent transformation, 91

Author Index